WITH
GREAT
PLEASURE

WITH GREAT PLEASURE

An Anthology of Poetry and Prose from the BBC Radio 4 Programme

EDITED BY ALEC REID

HUTCHINSON

LONDON MELBOURNE AUCKLAND JOHANNESBURG

© Introduction and selection Alec Reid 1986

An imprint of Century Hutchinson Ltd,
62-65 Chandos Place, London WC2N 4NW

Century Hutchinson Australia Pty Ltd
PO Box 496, 16-22 Church Street, Hawthorn, Melbourne, Victoria 3122,
Australia

Century Hutchinson New Zealand Limited
PO Box 40-086, Glenfield, Auckland 10, New Zealand

Century Hutchinson South Africa (Pty) Limited
PO Box 337, Bergvlei 2012, South Africa

First published 1986
Reprinted 1987

British Library Cataloguing in Publication Data
With great pleasure.
  1. With great pleasure (Radio program)
  I. Reid, Alec
  791.44'72   SPN1991.77.W5/

ISBN 0 09 167120 6

Photoset by Rowland Phototypesetting Ltd
Bury St Edmunds, Sufolk
Printed and bound in Great Britain by
Anchor Brendon Ltd, Tiptree, Essex

CONTENTS

ACKNOWLEDGEMENTS

Going, Going reprinted by permission of Faber and Faber Ltd from 'High Windows' by PHILIP LARKIN

A Lament for Moira McCavendish and *A Ballad of Investiture 1969* reprinted by permission of John Murray (Publishers) Ltd from 'Collected Poems' by JOHN BETJEMAN

But Murderous by STEVIE SMITH from 'The Collected Poems of Stevie Smith' published by Penguin Modern Classics, reproduced by permission of James MacGibbon

Waste and *Billy* by HARRY GRAHAM from 'Ruthless Rhymes for Heartless Homes' published by E. J. Arnold Ltd

The Thousandth Man by RUDYARD KIPLING from 'Rudyard Kipling's Verse' reproduced by permission of A. P. Watt Ltd on behalf of The National Trust and Macmillan London Ltd

Extract from *Advice to a Lecturer* by MICHAEL FARADAY reproduced by courtesy of the Royal Institution

Extract from *Beginning Again* by LEONARD WOOLF reproduced by permission of the author's Estate and Chatto & Windus: The Hogarth Press

Eight O' Clock and extract from *A Shropshire Lad* from 'Collected Poems' by A. E. HOUSEMAN reproduced by permission of The Society of Authors (as the literary representative of the Estate of A. E. Houseman) and Jonathan Cape Ltd

The Thirty-Ninth Rose by ERIC WALTER WHITE published privately 1977 and reproduced by permission of Sarah White

The Psychology of Shakespeare from 'The State of Psychiatry' by AUBREY LEWIS reproduced by permission of Routledge & Kegan Paul Ltd

To Hedli from '85 Poems' by LOUIS MACNEICE published by Faber and Faber Ltd and reproduced by permission of David Higham Associates Ltd

Her Triumph, The Pity of Love and *September 1913* by W. B. YEATS reproduced by permission of A. P. Watt Ltd on behalf of Michael Yeats and Macmillan London Ltd

FOREWORD

This book celebrates 'With Great Pleasure', a programme which has been running successfully for over fifteen years on Radio 4. A person, generally prominent in the arts or in public life, presents in some hall, theatre or studio, a selection of his or her favourite poetry and prose. Reading the items to the assembled audience are an actor and actress.

On the face of it nothing could be simpler, but it is often the simplest ideas that need the most careful thought. In a less unjust world it would not be me compiling this anthology, but my predecessor, the late Brian Patten, a gifted and much loved producer with the BBC in Bristol. Although the series came into existence in 1970 every programme was produced by a different person and it tended to be somewhat untidy in form, with some presenters both introducing and reading the whole selection – a feat which few could bring off with any conviction – and others with just one actor of the same sex reading with them, leading in the end to a sameness of sound little different from the solo performances. It was Brian in the mid 1970s who – along with his assistant Margaret Bradley, now a producer in her own right – took the whole thing over, lent it a style and ensured its continuing popularity. It is a programme in which people like to be invited to appear. After all, the chance to share a lifetime's reading, a lifetime's enthusiasms is almost irresistible. The shock comes sometimes when the presenter realises that the well-remembered poem is not, after all, remembered word for word, that the novel which changed his life contains no passage that can be lifted to stand on its own, and did he, in any case, want to re-read the whole thing just then? Many a time I have been told, 'Well, it was great fun, but I never realised it would be such hard work.' By telling you this, I have no wish to discourage potential contributors – the other side of the coin is that the actual recording tends to be extremely pleasurable for all concerned. Whenever possible we go to some town or village with which the presenter is connected, where he or she was brought up, say, or where he or she has laid down roots. In consequence the local audience is generally warmly disposed towards the participants. It is invidious to single out individual programmes, so in citing Sir Peter Pears' programme as illustration of the latter point I do so because the recording took place only last week and it is upper-most in my mind. The affection the audience in the Jubilee Hall at Aldeburgh had for him raised the temperature of a chilly January day by several degrees. This of course added to the pleasure of the evening for him and for us, and, ultimately, for the listener at home.

There have now been well over 160 programmes and of course over the years a number of items have proved popular with both presenters and listeners. Indeed, tactful negotiation occasionally has to take place to ensure that the same poem does not occur more than once in the same series. One of the more requested items, not included in this anthology, is Rupert Brooke's 'The Old Vicarage, Grantchester', and for the sake of the audience I have to limit its appearance to no more than once every couple of series or so. In general, however, there are no restrictions as to choice placed on the presenters. After all, we are inviting them to share with us what has given *them* most pleasure.

In selecting for this book I was placed in somewhat of a dilemma. Should I concentrate on the items most often included on the air? I decided in the end not to make that the basis for selection, if only on the grounds that they are almost certainly readily available elsewhere and you probably already have them. At the same time there would be no point in making the book totally unrepresentative of the series as a whole. So how about a 'Best Of . . . ?' Totally impossible as the book would then almost certainly be over 160 programmes long! I realised in the end that I was in a uniquely favoured position, in that whereas the people I invite to take part are constrained by the almost impossible task of having to distil a lifetime's reading into forty-five minutes, I have been given the equivalent of eighteen hours or so to present from the programmes pieces that I have particularly enjoyed and which in very many cases were new discoveries for me. Some pieces that I have included also because every time they are broadcast we receive dozens of letters from people requesting information as to where it is possible to obtain a copy. I will be pleased to direct them to this volume.

I have made a point also of including some items which have rarely if ever been published, for instance a piece of Chaucer discovered by a colleague of Sir Lawrence Bragg's and included in his programme, or a letter of proposal to one of Steve Race's ancestors which must have been totally resistible at the time and which is now totally charming and funny.

As its producer, the programme provides me with opportunities to meet many of those whom I have admired and enjoyed in their public capacities and to get to know them a little better as people. It is a privileged position and I am grateful for it. It is with great pleasure that I share it with you.

Alec Reid
January 1986

KINGSLEY AMIS

1980

The affability, the fondness for whisky and the insistence on the correct use of language and pronounciation, these were to be expected. What did surprise me was Kingsley Amis's relish for sending himself up. In the break between the rehearsal and the recording of 'With Great Pleasure' we conducted a spoof interview for an April Fool programme I was producing for Radio 3. It concerned a non-existent poet called Brian Alexander (an amalgam of my name and that of the writer, Brian Sibley) who was purported after one of his readings to have thrown the distinguished novelist, who had happened to be in the audience, down the stairs. With remarkable generosity of spirit, Amis agreed to take part in the 'documentary' and to analyse Alexander's appeal. Entering into the spirit of the thing, he looked at the poems, which were in fact slightly improved adolescent verses of Brian's, and said to me, 'Well, which of my lines do you want me to take – "I really don't go much for all this modern rubbish" or "It's good to see someone struggling with traditional forms these days"?' He then proceeded to deliver a shrewd and extremely funny extempore review.

Let's begin with a poem I came across as a schoolboy. It showed me two things: one, that poetry could be as exciting as Louis Armstrong, whose works I was discovering at about the same time, and two, that poetry wasn't remote and high-flown, or needn't be; it could be very much of the time and place I was living in. Later I found that the poet, Francis Thompson, was a bad guy, that he was sentimental and sensationalist and anyway

13

out of fashion. Later still I forgot all that and saw that although 'The Kingdom of God' wasn't the greatest poem in the world, as I'd once thought, it was pretty good for all that. The very well-known phrase that comes in the middle is Thompson's invention as far as I know.

The Kingdom of God
FRANCIS THOMPSON

O world invisible, we view thee,
O world intangible, we touch the,
O world unknowable, we know thee,
Inapprehensible, we clutch thee.

Does the fish soar to find the ocean,
The eagle plunge to find the air –
That we ask of the stars in motion
If they have rumour of thee there?

Not where the wheeling systems darken,
And our benumbed conceiving soars! –
The drift of pinions, would we hearken,
Beats at our own clay-shuttered doors.

The angels keep their ancient places; –
Turn but a stone, and start a wing!
'Tis ye, 'tis your estranged faces,
That miss the many-splendoured thing.

But (when so sad thou canst not sadder)
Cry; – and upon thy so sore loss
Shall shine the traffic of Jacob's ladder
Pitched betwixt Heaven and Charing Cross.

Yea, in the night, my Soul, my daughter,
Cry, – clinging Heaven by the hems;
And lo, Christ walking on the water,
Not of Gennesareth, but Thames!

One man who was completely out in my schooldays and later, out in a bigger way than Thompson could ever have been, was Tennyson. No insult was too big for him: he was hypocritical,

superficial, smug, patriotic (a deadly sin), stupid and, worst
of all, Victorian. That was a long time ago; it's interesting to see
how that word 'Victorian' has changed from being a term of
abuse to denoting envious approval, so that people talk about
the Victorian values of stability and domesticity. Anyway,
Victorian or not, and I think not in a lot of ways, Tennyson
was a poet of stupendous natural talent: not even Keats sur-
passed him in that. He said of himself that other men had written
better poetry than his, but none had written poetry that sounded
better. Correct. Here's one of the songs from his verse play, *The
Princess*:

Come Down O Maid
ALFRED, LORD TENNYSON

'Come down, O maid from yonder mountain height:
What pleasure lives in height (The shepherd sang)
In height and cold, the splendour of the hills?
But cease to move so near the Heavens, and cease
To glide a sunbeam by the blasted Pine,
To sit a star upon the sparkling spire;
And come, for Love is of the valley, come,
For Love is of the valley, come thou down
And find him; by the happy threshold, he,
Or hand in hand with plenty in the maize,
Or red with spirted purple of the vats,
Or foxlike in the vine; nor cares to walk
With Death and Morning on the silver horns,
Nor wilt thou snare him in the white ravine,
Nor find him dropt upon the firths of ice,
That huddling slant in furrow-cloven falls
To roll the torrent out of dusky doors:
But follow; let the torrent dance thee down
To find him in the valley; let the wild
Lean-headed Eagles yelp alone, and leave
The monstrous ledges there to slope, and spill
Their thousand wreaths of dangling water-smoke,
That like a broken purpose waste in air:
So waste not thou; but come; for all the vales
Await thee; azure pillars of the hearth

15

Arise to thee; the children call, and I
Thy shepherd pipe, and sweet is every sound,
Sweeter they voice, but every sound is sweet;
Myriads of rivulets hurrying through the lawn,
The moan of doves in immemorial elms,
And murmuring of innumerable bees.'

I was lucky enough to be a contemporary of Philip Larkin at Oxford and have never quite recovered from my surprise at finding that that beer-drinking, jazz-loving breaker of college rules was also a most sensitive and exquisite poet, in the true senses of those terms. He didn't always write in that mood or that style; he had a tougher, more direct manner, well illustrated in a poem he wrote on a commission from the Department of the Environment, if you can believe such a thing. It was first published about fifteen years ago, and since then things have certainly gone the way he said they would.

Going, Going
PHILIP LARKIN

I thought it would last my time –
The sense that, beyond the town,
There would always be fields and farms,
Where the village louts could climb
Such trees as were not cut down;
I knew there'd be false alarms

In the papers about old streets
And split level shopping, but some
Have always been left so far;
And when the old parts retreat
As the bleak high-risers come
We can always escape in the car.

Things are tougher than we are, just
As earth will always respond
However we mess it about;
Chuck filth in the sea, if you must:
The tides will be clean beyond.
– But what do I feel now? Doubt?

Or age, simply? The crowd
Is young in the M1 cafe;
Their kids are screaming for more –
More houses, more parking allowed,
More caravan sites, more pay.
On the business page, a score

Of spectacled grins approve
Some takeover bid that entails
Five per cent profits (and ten
Per cent more in the estuaries): move
Your works to unspoilt dales
(Grey area grants)! And when

You try to get near the sea
In summer . . .
                              It seems, just now,
To be happening so very fast;
Despite all the land left free
For the first time I feel somehow
That it isn't going to last,

That before I snuff it, the whole
Boiling will be bricked in
Except for the tourist parts –
First slum of Europe: a role
It won't be so hard to win,
With a cast of crooks and tarts.

And that will be England gone,
The shadows, the meadows, the lanes,
The guildhalls, the carved choirs.
There'll be books; it will linger on
In galleries; but all that remains
For us will be concrete and tyres.

Most things are never meant.
This won't be, most likely: but greeds
And garbage are too thick strewn
To be swept up now, or invent
Excuses that make them all needs.
I just think it will happen soon.

No programme of writings that give me pleasure would be anything else but disastrously incomplete without something by John Betjeman. In a time when so many public figures are monsters or frauds it was nice to come across one who thoroughly deserved his popularity. He's probably the last poet to have commanded anything like a mass audience in the manner of Tennyson, whom he greatly admired and whose work had something in common with his own, mastery of sound, for example. Where Betjeman was quite different, indeed unique, was his ability to move from something pleasantly light, even comic, to painful emotions like grief and remorse, and to do it quite smoothly, without any noticeable change of key. So in the next poem, *A Lament for Moira McCavendish*, we begin in a spirit of gentle fun and then find ourselves plunged into sorrow and a sense of loss; very characteristic of this splendid poet.

A Lament For Moira McCavendish
JOHN BETJEMAN

Through the midlands of Ireland I journeyed by diesel
    And bright in the sun shone the emerald plain;
Though loud sang the birds on the thorn-bush and teasel
    They could not be heard for the sound of the train.

The roll of the railway made musing creative:
    I thought of the colleen I soon was to see
With her wiry black hair and grey eyes of the native,
    Sweet Moira McCavendish, Acushla Machree.

Her brother's wee cabin stands distant from Tallow
    A league and a half, where the Blackwater flows,
And the musk and potato, the mint and the mallow
    Do grow there in beauty, along with the rose.

'Twas smoothly we raced through the open expansion
    Of rush-covered levels and gate-lodge and gate
And the ruined demesne and the windowless mansion
    Where once the oppressor had revelled in state.

At Castletownriche, as the prospect grew hillier,
    I saw the far mountains to Moira long-known
Till I came to the valley and townland familiar
    With the Protestant church standing locked and alone.

18

O vein of my heart! upon Tallow Road Station
   No face was to greet me, so freckled and white;
As the diesel slid out, leaving still desolation,
   The McCavendish ass-cart was nowhere in sight.

For a league and half to the Blackwater river
   I tramped with my bundle her cabin to see
And herself by the fuchsias, her young lips a-quiver
   Half-smiling, half-weeping a welcome to me.

Och Moira McCavendish! the fangs of the creeper
   Have struck at the thatch and thrust open the door;
The couch in the garden grows ranker and deeper
   Than musk and potato which bloomed there before.

Flow on, you remorseless and salmon-full waters!
   What care I for prospects so silvery fair?
The heart in me's dead, like your sweetest of daughters,
   And I would that my spirit were lost on the air.

Readers: Judi Dench, Tim Pigott-Smith

Full Selection:
The Kingdom of God, FRANCIS THOMPSON
Come Down O Maid, ALFRED, LORD TENNYSON
Going, Going, PHILIP LARKIN
Don't Miss This, PETER SIMPLE
The Runnable Stag, JOHN DAVIDSON
The Cuirassiers of the Frontier, ROBERT GRAVES
Act of Faith, IRWIN SHAW
A Lament for Moira McCavendish, JOHN BETJEMAN
Exposure, WILFRED OWEN
That Hideous Strength, C. S. LEWIS
The Gods of the Copybook Headings, RUDYARD KIPLING
Right Ho, Jeeves, P. G. WODEHOUSE
Fancy's Knell, A. E. HOUSMAN
The Rolling English Road, G. K. CHESTERTON

LINDSAY ANDERSON

1984

He won't remember the first time we met. It was during 1973 in the stalls of the Royal Court Theatre. As a producer attached to Radio Four's arts magazine programme, 'Kaleidoscope', I was sent to report on the Court's plans for the forthcoming season. As I was about to leave, I saw Lindsay Anderson standing on his own and, full of youthful enthusiasm – 'Kaleidoscope' was at that time a very new programme – asked if I might interview him. After looking me up and down for what seemed a considerable time, he finally said 'Ah well, I suppose you could do with a leg-up in your career.' That early impression of waspishness was for me totally dispelled on our second meeting, for the recording of 'With Great Pleasure', He was relaxed and friendly, full of professional courtesy and genuine warmth. It turned out to be one of the most enjoyable of any of the series I have worked on to date, and not just because the evening ended with all of us drinking on the lawns of Balliol College at midnight.

It is impossible to start on a programme of this kind without asking oneself 'Why?' I mean why did I, for instance, let myself in for it? Vanity and self display of course enter into it, but also the desire to share, to let people know about some works that have been a part of one's thinking and which perhaps they don't know and will enjoy, or be affected by too.

It may well be my classical background – I did Latin and Greek as a schoolboy and in fact came up to this very university, though not to Balliol, but to Wadham round the corner, on classics –

returning to Oxford from the war I'm afraid I lapsed into English literature – but I have still clung, I hope, to the classical ideas of lucidity, directness of communication, clarity of thought; and these are the qualities I like in poetry. I am not good at modern, should I say contemporary, poetry but the modern poets I like tend to be quirky, like Stevie Smith for instance. Here is a characteristic piece of hers in caustic common sense rather than whimsical mood.

But Murderous
STEVIE SMITH

A mother slew her unborn babe
In a day of recent date
Because she did not wish him to be born in a world
Of murder and war and hate
'Oh why should I bear a babe from my womb
To be broke in pieces by the hydrogen bomb?'

I say this woman deserves little pity
That she was a fool and a murderess
Is a child's destiny to be contained by a mind
That signals only a lady in distress

And why should human infancy be so superior
As to be too good to be born in this world?
Did she think it was an angel or a baa-lamb
That lay in her belly furled?

Oh the child is the young of its species
Alike with that noble, vile, curious and fierce
How foolish this poor mother to suppose
Her act told us aught that was not murderous

(As, item, That the arrogance of a half-baked mind
Breeds murder; makes us all unkind.)

I have to admit that with the years my attitude to my fellow men has grown more sardonic. They are really a rum lot. I don't think of myself as cynical – cynics prefer to think of themselves as realists – but I do have to admit to being unable to read a newspaper today or watch the news on television without a certain amount of revulsion. There is a verse that expresses the feeling perfectly by Walter Raleigh, not *the* Sir Walter Ralegh, but an Edwardian literatus.

I Wish I Loved the Human Race
WALTER RALEIGH

I wish I loved the human race
I wished I loved its silly face
I wish I loved the way it walks
I wish I loved the way it talks
And when I'm introduced to one
I wish I thought what jolly fun.

In this mood I am fond of repeating to myself a selection of Harry Graham's *'Ruthless Rhymes for Heartless Homes'*. They provide a healthy tonic, I think, against conventional sentimentalism. Here are two of my favourites.

Waste
HARRY GRAHAM

I had written to Aunt Maud
Who was on a trip abroad
When I heard she'd died of cramp
Just too late to save the stamp.

Billy

Billy, in one of his nice new sashes
Fell in the fire and was burned to ashes
Now, although the room grows chilly
I haven't the heart to poke poor Billy.

Ah yes, rhymers, scepticism, cynicism – call it anything you like – is dangerously attractive. I know one has to be careful or it slips into facility, but in a world so full of falsity, realism is surely beneficial as well as attractive.

It's a commonplace that as we get older we become more conservative, ever more reactionary. When I was young in the heady days of post-war Britain, I suppose I could be called an idealist, though hopeful was really a better word. I was certainly labelled an angry young man, and even a socialist. I wore a leather jacket and that was enough to label you a Brechtian. Well in fact I would never have called myself a socialist because I have always been too sceptical of centralised power. I've certainly found, and still find, a lot to be angry about, but I had great sympathy with the aristocratic ideal, with the sense of individual moral responsibility that goes with it and its mistrust of facile egalitarianism. Not fashionable. This brings me to another writer I'm always fond of dipping into and like to carry around with me. Henry Frederick Amiel was a Swiss-French intellectual and literatus whose sixty years of life spanned the middle of the last century. He wrote a journal, a chronicle of reflections and observation which was once celebrated, and which now no one seems to have read or heard of. *Amiel's Journal* is full of wisdom, the kind of wisdom I've been talking about. Not fashionable. Here for instance are some remarks of his on equality. Could it be called the twentieth century heresy?

Amiel's Journal

The modern leveller, after having done away with conventional inequalities, with arbitrary privilege and historical injustice, goes still further and rebels against the inequalities of merit, capacity and virtue. Beginning with a just principle he develops it into an unjust one. Inequality may be as true and as just as equality; it depends on what you mean by it, but this is precisely what nobody cares to find out. All passions dread the light and the modern zeal for equality is a disguised hatred which tries to pass itself off for love.

And the continuation . . .

Liberty, equality; bad principles, the only true principle for humanity is justice. And justice towards the feeble becomes necessarily protection or kindness.

'Liberty, equality; bad principles.' It would take some courage to say that on television today, or maybe even on radio. Only Enoch Powell at his best, I suppose could have got away with it. Here is another reflection from Amiel which I think provides a very direct

23

and necessary comment on the characteristics of contemporary sophistication, what Amiel calls cultivated society, and this was written I suppose about a hundred years ago.

If ignorance and passion are the foes of popular morality, moral indifference is the malady of the cultivated classes. The modern separation of enlightenment and virtue, of thought and conscience, of the intellectual aristocracy from the honest and vulgar crowd is the greatest danger that can threaten liberty. Our cynics and railers are mere egotists who stand aloof from the common duty and are of no service to society against any ill that may attack it. Their cultivation consists in having got rid of feeling, and thus they fall further and further away from true humanity and approach nearer to the demonical nature. What was it that Mephistopheles lacked? Not intelligence certainly, but goodness.

I'd like to leave you with a quotation to identify if you can. Who said, and where, and why, 'We go further. I am well and happy.'?

Readers: Jill Bennett, Frank Grimes

Full Selection:
The Municipal Gallery Revisited, W. B. YEATS
But Murderous, STEVIE SMITH
Autumn Journal, Section IX, LOUIS MACNEICE
I Wish I Loved the Human Race, SIR WALTER A. RALEIGH
Waste, HARRY GRAHAM
Billy, HARRY GRAHAM
On the Birth of His Son from ARTHUR WALEY'S translation of 170 Chinese poems
The Scholar Recruit, POW CHOU from above
Sailing Homeward from above
Out of Africa, KAREN BLIXEN
Amiel's Journal
God Is an Englishman, DONALD BORNE
Brief Quotations from JOHN DONNE, JOYCE CAREY, HENRY FIELDING, JEAN JACQUES ROUSSEAU, JOHN KEATS, KAREN BLIXEN and YURI GAGARIN
The Memoirs of Shostakovitch

Poem from *The Farm*, DAVID STOREY
Prater Violet, CHRISTOPHER ISHERWOOD
Red River Valley (song)

JEFFREY ARCHER

1984

At the time of writing, Jeffrey Archer had put aside for a time his career as a novelist to become deputy chairman of the Conservative Party. For the press it seemed as if it had suddenly become the Glorious Twelfth with Jeffrey as chief grouse. My own first impression of him was of an amiable, even kind man possessed of a pushy intelligence. There was on occasion a surprising element of self-deprecation. That may have been calculated, but what wasn't – and it made me warm to him further – was the revelation that he had included Kipling's 'The Thousandth Man' in appreciation of a friend who had stood by him during the worst of his financial troubles.

I have often heard it said that young people introduced to Shakespeare don't enjoy it because they either meet up with it too young or fail to appreciate its value. One of the great privileges I had at school was being taught by a man called Alan Quilter, now the Headmaster of Wells Cathedral School in Somerset, where I come from. He instilled in me a love of Shakespeare from a very young age. This piece I have chosen is one that shook me when I was young; it is of Richard II showing that he is the king. I couldn't believe that any man believed he would be a god or above all men, but this speech leaves one in absolutely no doubt.

Richard II
WILLIAM SHAKESPEARE

K. RICHARD. (To Northumberland) We are amaz'd;
And thus long have we stood
To watch the fearful bending of thy knee,
Because we thought ourself thy lawful king:
And if we be, how dare thy joints forget
To pay their awful duty to our presence?
If we be not, show us the hand of God
That hath dismiss'd us from our stewardship;
For well we know, no hand of blood and bone
Can gripe the sacred handle of our sceptre,
Unless he do profane, steal or usurp.
And though you think that all, as you have done,
Have torn their souls by turning them from us,
And we are barren and bereft of friends;
Yet know, my master, God omnipotent,
Is mustering in his clouds on our behalf
Armies of pestilence; and they shall strike
Your children yet unborn and unbegot,
That lift your vassal hands against my head
And threat the glory of my precious crown.
Tell Bolingbroke, – for yond methinks he stands, –
That every stride he makes upon my land
Is dangerous treason: he is come to ope
The purple testament of bleeding war;
But ere the crown he looks for live in peace,
Ten thousand bloody crowns of mothers' sons
Shall ill become the flower of England's face,
Change the complexion of her maid-pale peace
To scarlet indignation, and bedew
Her pastures' grass with faithful English blood.

When I came to live in London, I took a great interest in the theatre and there are certain plays that remain fixed in my memory. I remember Laurence Olivier's *Long Day's Journey Into Night*, I remember Alan Badel's *Kean* and I also remember my introduction to *The Relapse* by John Vanbrugh: Donald Sinden's performance, at the Royal Shakespeare Company when it was at the Aldwych, of the marvellous part of Lord Foppington, a character I always thought of as rather courageous as well as just being fun, as indeed were the women that surrounded him.

The Relapse
JOHN VANBRUGH

AMANDA. Nay, I love a neat library, too; but 'tis, I think, the inside of the book should recommend it most to us.

LORD FOPPINGTON. That, I must confess, I am nat altogether so fand of. Far to my mind the inside of a book, is to entertain one's self with the forced product of another man's brain. Naw I think a man of quality and breeding may be much better diverted with the natural sprauts of his own. But to say the truth, madam, let a man love reading never so well, when once he comes to know this tawn, he finds so many better ways of passing the four-and-twenty hours, that 'twere ten thousand pities he should consume his time in that. Far example, madam, my life; my life, madam, is a perpetual stream of pleasure, that glides through such a variety of entertainments, I believe the wisest of our ancestors never had the least conception of any of 'em. I rise, madam, about ten a-clack. I don't rise sooner, because 'tis the worst thing in the world for the complexion; nat that I pretend to be a beau; but a man must endeavour to look wholesome, lest he make so nauseous a figure in the side-bax, the ladies should be compelled to turn their eyes upon the play. So at ten a-clack, I say, I rise. Naw, if I find 'tis a good day, I resalve to take a turn in the Park, and see the fine women; so huddle on my clothes, and get dressed by one. If it be nasty weather, I take a turn in the chocolate-haus: where, as you walk, madam, you have the prettiest prospect in the world; you have looking glasses all round you. – But I'm afraid I tire the company.

BERINTHIA. Not at all. Pray go on,

LORD FOPPINGTON. Why then, Ladies, from thence I go to dinner at Lacket's, where you are so nicely and delicately served, that, stap my vitals, they shall compose you a dish no bigger than a saucer, shall come to fifty shillings. Between eating my dinner (and washing my mauth, ladies) I spend my time, 'till I go to the play; where 'till nine a-clack, I entertain myself with looking upon the company, and usually dispose of one hour more in leading 'em aut. So there's twelve of the four-and-twenty pretty well over. The other twelve, madam, are disposed of in two articles: in the first four I toast myself drunk, and in t'other eight I sleep myself sober again. Thus, ladies, you see my life is an eternal round O of delights.

I have always been moved by the poet and writer Rudyard Kipling, probably because my father was a soldier and the great traditions he stood for I think are still worth standing for today. It's a nice touch that Alec (McCowen) is actually playing Kipling here at the Mermaid theatre. He told me that many people have written to him and asked him why he left this great poem out – to which he replied again and again that it would have been an eight or nine-hour performance if he had included everything that everybody wanted. None the less it is still a magnificent poem; it's called 'The Thousandth Man' and in it we see everything we expect from our closest friends.

The Thousandth Man
RUDYARD KIPLING

One man in a thousand, Solomon says,
Will stick more close than a brother.
And it's worth while seeking him half your days
If you find him before the other.
Nine hundred and ninety-nine depend
On what the world sees in you,
But the Thousandth Man will stand your friend
With the whole round world agin you.

'Tis neither promise nor prayer nor show
Will settle the finding for 'ee.
Nine hundred and ninety-nine of 'em go
By your looks, or your acts, or your glory.
But if he finds you and you find him,
The rest of the world don't matter;
For the Thousandth Man will sink or swim
With you in any water.

You can use his purse with no more talk
Than he uses yours for his spendings,
And laugh and meet in your daily walk
As though there had been no lendings.
Nine hundred and ninety-nine of 'em call
For silver and gold in their dealings;
But the Thousandth Man he's worth 'em all,
Because you can show him your feelings.

His wrong's your wrong, and his right's your right,
In season or out of season.
Stand up and back it in all men's sight –
With *that* for your only reason!
Nine hundred and ninety-nine can't bide
The shame or mocking or laughter,
But the Thousandth Man will stand by your side
To the gallows-foot – and after!

Readers: Judi Dench, Alec McCowen

Full selection:
Matilda, Who Told Lies, and Was Burned to Death, HILLAIRE BELLOC
Burial of Sir John Moore after Corunna, CHARLES WOLFE
Richard II, Act III, Scene III, WILLIAM SHAKESPEARE
Inaugural Address of President Kennedy, J. F. KENNEDY
Romeo and Juliet, Act IV, Scene III, WILLIAM SHAKESPEARE
The Relapse, JOHN VANBRUGH
The American Constitution, (Declaration of Independence) 1776
The Prodigy, HERMAN HESSE
Call for The Dead, JOHN LE CARRÉ
The Old Vicarage, Grantchester, RUPERT BROOKE
London Telephone Directory A–D
The Sensible Thing, F. SCOTT FITZGERALD
Arthur Wellard (1902–1980), HAROLD PINTER
A Midsummer Night's Dream, WILLIAM SHAKESPEARE

DAVID BELLAMY

1981

Bellamy's joy in life virtually leaps from the page. It seems wholly appropriate that when including a poem of Rupert Brooke's, he should choose 'The Great Lover', a celebration of the senses. With such joy is linked, inevitably, energy. Many of the hosts of 'With Great Pleasure' select a passage from the Bible, usually something to do with peace and understanding; in Bellamy's case it was the parable of the talents. As a teacher he sees his responsibility as helping a student find what is relevant to him or her: 'When somebody finds what is relevant to them, they find their talent and off they go.' He finds some amusement that his talent should have been that of a naturalist: 'I wish I could have sung tenor, or been as good as Nureyev in the ballet – that would have been a talent.' Another talent he possesses, he didn't mention directly, that of professional communicator, but he used it effectively in the programme to put the case for what springs from his love of his surroundings, that of conservation.

I can't think of anything which would give me more pleasure than to sit on a beautiful, sunny summer's evening in a place like the Bowes Museum, which is ultra-Victorian, and be read all my favourite poems and prose by two extremely talented people. And I really am a Victorian at heart; I always think I was born about a hundred years too late. But I must also add that I'd like to have been an 'up-market' Victorian: I'd like to have been the guy who actually built this place, rather than perhaps the guy who had to work out there.

First memories of the countryside: and the first countryside I knew was deep in the heart of Surrey, a little place called Spring Pond, and it was so private and so exciting to that I didn't really want anybody else to know where it was. But there was a pond there, fed by a spring. My big brother and I used to build rafts, we would go across it on those rafts, and it was the whole world. And there at the end of the pond were some rhododendrons – you could go behind the rhododendrons and you could have been anywhere; it was to me total excitement. It was exploring a cool, wet, green, wonderfully smelling world, that damp and thrilling smell that we living out in the country here all know so well, but then I didn't.

And I can well remember going collecting whortleberries or bilberries or windberries, they have so many different common names. I used to go with my Granny and she was the best berry-picker of the lot. Along she would go and all her bag would be full and my mouth would be full and I wouldn't have very many in my bag at all.

I remember one day she turned round – we were in deep bracken – and she was holding an adder in her hand, and she said, 'What a pretty stick', and then realised. That is the magic of the countryside, because if you know what you are doing then you are safe, and if you don't know what you are doing you do it with complete naivity and I'm quite sure you're still safe. That snake knew just as well as I did that Granny was a townsperson, that she didn't really know what she was doing.

So, Spring Pond Cottage – my first look at the countryside, my first real adventure, one of the first things I really learned to love. It brings me to my favourite poet, Rupert Brooke, and his poem 'The Great Lover'.

The Great Lover
RUPERT BROOKE

These I have loved:
>   White plates and cups, clean gleaming,
Ringed with blue lines; and feathery, faery dust;
Wet roofs, beneath the lamp-light; the strong crust
Of friendly bread; and many-tasting food;
Rainbows; and the blue bitter smoke of wood;

And radiant raindrops couching in cool flowers;
And flowers themselves, that sway through sunny hours,
Dreaming of moths that drink them under the moon;
Then, the cool kindliness of sheets, that soon
Smooth away trouble; and the rough male kiss
Of blankets; grainy wood; live hair that is
Shining and free; blue-massing clouds; the keen
Unpassioned beauty of a great machine;
The benison of hot water; furs to touch;
The good smell of old clothes; and other such –
The comfortable smell of friendly fingers,
Hair's fragrance, and the musty reek that lingers
About dead leaves and last year's ferns . . .
And washen stones, gay for an hour; the cold
Graveness of iron; moist black earthen mould;
Sleep; and high places; footprints in the dew;
And oaks; and brown horse-chestnuts, glossy-new;
And new-peeled sticks; and shining pools on grass; –
All these have been my loves. And these shall pass,
Whatever passes not, in the great hour,
Nor all my passion, all my prayers, have power
To hold them with me through the gate of Death.
They'll play deserter, turn with the traitor breath,
Break the high bond we made, and sell Love's trust
And sacramented covenant to the dust.
– Oh, never a doubt but, somewhere, I shall wake,
And give what's left of love again, and make
New friends, now strangers . . .
                              But the best I've known
Stays here, and changes, breaks, grows old, is blown
About the winds of the world, and fades from brains
Of living men, and dies.
                              Nothing remains.

O dear my loves, O faithless, once again
This one last gift I give; that after men
Shall know, and later lovers, far-removed,
Praise you, 'All these were lovely'; say, 'He loved'.

I can't think of anything in that poem which I don't myself love, that I haven't a great love for. He mentions it all. I tried to sit down and think of other things and put in other lines, which is pretty terrible when you're looking at a poet such as that. But one always must remember that Rupert Brooke gave his life in the War, gave his life to this thing which is the British Isles – I think more than anything that means most to me – this diversity, yet uniformity. Let's go perhaps to my favourite poem of all, 'The Old Vicarage, Grantchester', which is about the Cambridgeshire landscape. In it he says he's speaking from Germany where he's serving in the army:

> Here tulips bloom as they are told;
> Unkempt about those hedges blows
> An English unofficial rose.

And that's it: we still have an unofficial countryside, a country-side which criss-crosses and holds together this highly pro-ductive machine on which we so depend. And as long as that semi-natural web-matrix is there, Britain will stay the same – productive, and looked after.

A great conflict has been raging with me in the last few years because I have had more and more letters saying 'how can you talk about evolution and also say you are a Christian?' I must have had three thousand letters during the running of 'Botanic Man' on television saying I was a wicked man – 'Bellamy and Attenborough are cast on the anvil of the Devil. If it wasn't for men like these our churches would be full to overflowing', that sort of thing. I want to state why I can believe in both. I believe in God and it doesn't matter whether it's our God, there are plenty of other Gods worshipped just as religiously and fervently and with just as much devotion across this world of ours. But God created a law – a law which governs the interaction between matter and energy. Einstein showed us that they were both but two forms of the same thing. Once that law, which basically says that wherever there is energy, wherever there is potential it will be used, had been created – evolution had to happen. This whole complex thing had to happen, reaping the benefit of this planet Earth. Man has been set aside from all the other products of evolution not by the power of conscious thought, because whales and dolphins and I'm sure certain other organisms share that with us, but by free will.

And it is by the exercise of free will that we may disobey that law of the universe. We needn't use everything which is there; we can conserve; we can put things away for the future. Conservation is the sensible utilisation of natural resources. If we choose that we will survive. If we don't do that we will join other groups of animals that have taken too much – that have obeyed the law and not had the purposeful thing of free will. We will join them; we will follow them to extinction, to self-destruction.

The Shaping of Progress from The Human Experiment
W. GRAHAM SMITH

Men are the only conscious organising agents on this planet. If they are to perform this function satisfactorily, shaping progress rather than following where events blindly lead, then it is essential that we as individuals should understand the more important principles that underlie the behaviour of the world in which we live. These principles have been made known gradually by the collective efforts of mankind, largely as a result of the progress of science; some of them and their approximate interrelations have been noted in the present book. Unless individual men and women come to know the feel of the nature of things in this kind of way, and to apply this understanding, then we cannot hope to develop our world to good purpose, not least because it is a single interacting whole. At present however most of us are scarcely aware of the principles involved, and still less of their implications. It is argued that it is essential that we should modify our cultural approach in general, and our educational system in particular, with a view to overcoming this deficiency. Its accomplishment would involve changes in our outlook, in our forms of social organisation, in our relation to plants and animals, and to our environment as a whole. We would find ourselves able in due course to bring all these to interact with one another in a harmonious way and so produce a global setting that was essentially self-regulating and stable and would provide a healthy base that could support virtually infinite further qualitative growth. Progress along such lines would be broadly to the benefit of all men and women living on this planet; it is a goal towards which we can all work without conflict of interest, whatever our race or circumstances, in our conjoint endeavour to enable the creative potential inherent in the Universe to attain a full expression here on Planet Earth.

Can it be done? The answer is yes. And I will tell you why. Because somewhere in this mess we call the end of the twentieth century there are decent human beings trying to get out. The meek shall inherit the earth – if the meek don't get out pretty soon and become vociferous it is not going to be worth inheriting.

The next piece was an entry to a competition in the magazine *The Living Countryside*, and it was project No.6 in which the entrants were asked to define a project in their own area which would improve the environment. A ten-year-old little girl:

At our shopping parade there is a small area of grass which could be very nice because it has a seat on it – old people could sit there. But people walk across the grass and wear it out and so it gets dirty and water-logged, people leave litter, sweet papers, silver paper and old paper bags. I think there should be a small fence round the grass and a little bin and perhaps a tree should be planted, I think this might be possible by sending a letter such as 'Dear Sir, we are very concerned about the state of our corner. Is it possible that we can arrange to meet you to discuss how we can make improvements? Yours sincerely.'

That doesn't sound very important does it? But here is the letter that came with it:

Dear Sir, this notebook will arrive too late to be included in the competition. However, the child's brothers wish you to see her notebook and she herself would have wanted me to send it to you. Emily completed her notebook while in the last stages of terminal cancer. She persevered every week looking forward to each new issue of the magazine to see what that week's project contained. We got a bit stuck on project Number 5, because the only tree she could see from her bed was a very old gnarled plum. Similarly in Number 6, she could no longer get out of bed so sent her Daddy off to take photos of the small patch of grass. By the time we got to the last page she could no longer see what she was writing. The little notebook represents enormous courage and endurance by a child who was passionately fond of plants and wildlife and I felt you should all see it. I enclose a stamped addressed envelope for its return as it is very precious. Emily died a fortnight ago.

Now if there are children like that, and there are many – all over the world I meet people with that sort of caring knowledge – we can make it work.

Readers: Michele Dotrice, Dinsdale Landen

Full Selection:
Swallows and Amazons, ARTHUR RANSOME
The Way Through the Woods, RUDYARD KIPLING
The Great Lover, RUPERT BROOKE
The Naturalist on the Amazon, H. W. BATES
The Parable of the Talents
The Way that I Went, ROBERT LLOYD PRAEGER
The Courtship of the Yonghy-Bonghy-Bo, EDWARD LEAR
Mind in the Waters, J. MACINTYRE
Genesis 1–6
The Teacher, LESLIE PINCKNEY HILL
The Shaping of Progress, W. GRAHAM SMITH (From *The Human Experiment*)
Competition Letters
Chocolate Button Advertisement

ALAN BENNETT

1977

For all his delight in humour and pleasure in entertaining, his stylish analysis of the nature of programmes such as 'With Great Pleasure', much of Alan Bennett's selection appeared to highlight some of the sad resonances of English life, a sense of energy wasted: 'Diary of a Nobody', Auden's 'Musée des Beaux Arts', Stevie Smith's 'Not Waving But Drowning' and Philip Larkin's 'The Whitsun Wedding' where after the excitement and the conspiracy of women 'there swelled/A sense of falling . . .' Perversely the final impression is not of a pessimistic view of England or of mere nostalgia, but of a sort of weary optimism, as if under all the emotional dust the polish on the drawing-room furniture still shines.

I am being entertained.

My host sits me down, puts on a record and says, coyly, 'I think you're going to like this'.

I fix on my face an expression of what I hope will pass for appreciation. I even shake my head slowly as though granted a revelation of such beauty it's unbearable. Meanwhile he sits back with a look of immense self-satisfaction watching the spell work what he imagines is its old magic.

It can be pre-Columbian flute music. It can be Elton John. Either way it is a nightmare.

And I don't want to do that to you. I am not saying with each of the items I have chosen 'You'll like this. I do,' so much as 'I am the sort of person who likes this.' It is a form of self-revelation, even self-indulgence. It's a bit of a striptease. This was very well put by Kenneth Grahame, the author of *Wind in the Willows*.

You must please remember that a theme, a thesis, a subject, is in most cases little more than a sort of clothes line on which one pegs a string of ideas, quotations, allusions and so on, one's mental undergarments of all shapes and sizes, some probably fairly new, but most rather old and patched; and they dance and sway in the breeze and flap and flutter, or hang limp and lifeless, and some are ordinary enough, and some are of a rather private and intimate shape and rather give the owner away and show up his or her own peculiarities.

That is my side of it. Your side of it is summed up in a remark by Florence Nightingale.

What it is to be read aloud to. The most miserable exercise of the human intellect. It is like lying on one's back with one's hands tied and having liquid poured down one's throat.

When it comes to reading I am easily put off. I am put off a book if too many people like it. I am put off a book if some people like it too much.

Lewis Carroll is a case in point, Tolkien another. Both to some extent *picketed* by their admirers. I have never managed to read Wodehouse because I'm depressed by the enthusiasism of the people who do.

I am sure this is foolish and a failing on my part, but I'm also sure with books you're more likely to have a love-affair after a casual pick-up than after an 'I'm sure you two are going to get on like a house on fire' sort of introduction.

A book chooses its readers as a play chooses its audience. Fashion has something to do with it, but it's not fashion alone. Somewhere a voice is calling and if the wrong people respond it puts me off the author. I do not see his book. I do not see his play.

I am sure this applies to myself too and indeed when I sit in the audience at one of my own plays I often feel that's not where I belong. Had I not written it I probably shouldn't have gone to see it.

The public are often more interested in an author's life than in his or her work. Certainly this is true of Virginia Woolf and perhaps not so surprising since her novels are short on plot and without much humour. Her life on the other hand had plenty of both.

Beginning Again, an Autobiography of the Years 1911–1918
LEONARD WOOLF

Virginia and I were married on Saturday, August 10, at St Pancras Register Office in a room which, in those days, looked down into a cemetery. In the ceremony before a Registrar one makes no promise 'to love and to cherish, till death do us part, according to God's holy ordinance', but in the St Pancras Office, facing the window and looking through it at the tombstones behind the Registrar's head, one was, I suppose appropriately, reminded of the words 'till death do us part'. Apart from the tombstones, our wedding ceremony was provided with an element of comic relief (quite unintended) characteristic of the Stephens.

In the middle of the proceedings Vanessa (Virginia's sister) interrupted the Registrar, saying: 'Excuse me interrupting; I have just remembered: we registered my son – he is two years old – in the name of Clement, and we now want to change his name to Quentin. Can you tell me what we have to do?' There was a moment of astonished silence in the room as we all looked round sympathetically and saw the serious, slightly puzzled look on Vanessa's face. There was a pause while the Registrar stared at her with his mouth open. Then he said severely: 'One thing at a time, please, Madam.'

Readers: Alan Bennett, Phyllida Law

Full Selection:
Fetching Cows, NORMAN MAcCAIG
The Diary of a Nobody, GEORGE and WEEDON GROSSMITH
Denton Welch: A Selection from His Published Works edited by JOCELYN BROOKS
Musée des Beaux Arts, W. H. AUDEN

SIR JOHN BETJEMAN

1979

As Sir John is far and away the most requested modern poet, there is hardly an edition of 'With Great Pleasure' that does not include one of his poems, it was only a matter of time before my predecessor, Brian Patten, asked him to present his own selection. I met him a number of times whilst I was a studio manager, notably for the recordings of the Poetry Proms which were produced by George MacBeth and which featured Jill Balcon and Gary Watson as readers. My favourite memory, however, is of one of Sir John's programmes on the English Hymnal, produced by Religious Broadcasting. Assorted senior members of that department were fussing about in the studio, making a great display of welcome. Sir John let this continue for a while, but I could see he was amused. Suddenly he said, 'I say, do you think we could have some gin?', and produced a fiver from his trouser pocket. It was ten o'clock in the morning. There was much embarrassment, during which he was prevailed upon to put away his money and the boss left, sending a secretary in search of an off-licence. Sir John, the producer, the other studio manager and I then set about recording the programme which didn't take very long, though long enough for the gin to arrive. We were all sitting round the table, neat gin in paper cups, when Sir John produced a book, 'Have you seen the new

edition of Hardy? It's frightfully good.' He then proceeded to read us a
great many of the poems. It made for a delightful morning – after all, not
many jobs allow the possibility of a pleasant couple of hours being read
Hardy by the Poet Laureate. The remainder of the gin (there wasn't
much) was finally locked away in a cupboard somewhere in the bowels of
Religious Broadcasting.

Desmond McCarthy, I think it was, said that he was once staying
in a country house and Hardy was a fellow guest, and Hardy was
very quiet and when they went for a walk McCarthy said, 'Why
are you so quiet, don't you like these people?' And Hardy said,
'Oh, I like them, but I don't trust them.'

'Why don't you trust them?'

'I think they'll steal my plots,' Hardy said.

Hardy, apparently, set great store by his plots.

Her Second Husband Hears Her Story
THOMAS HARDY

'Still, Dear, it is incredible to me
    That here, alone,
You should have sewed him up until he died,
And in this very bed. I do not see
How you could do it, seeing what might betide.'

'Well, he came home one midnight, liquored deep –
    Worse than I'd known –
And lay down heavily, and soundly slept:
Then, desperate driven, I thought of it, to keep
Him from me when he woke. Being an adept

'With needle and thimble, as he snored, click-click
    An hour I'd sewn,
Till, had he roused, he couldn't have moved from bed,
So tightly laced in sheet and quilt and tick
He lay. And in the morning he was dead.

'Ere people came I drew the stitches out,
    And thus 'twas shown
To be a stroke.' – 'It's a strange tale!' said he.

41

'And this same bed?' – 'Yes, here it came about.'
'Well, it sounds strange – told here and now to me.

'Did you intend his death by your tight lacing?'
    'O, that I cannot own.
I could not think of else that would avail
When he should wake up, and attempt embracing.' –
    'Well, it's a cool queer tale!'

It most certainly is.

I can see how Ezra Pound was probably right when he said that Hardy's novels were really compressed into his poems.

And now we go to Cambridge, because the Lord of Language, for me, is Alfred Tennyson. And 'In Memoriam' I think contains his most beautiful poems. He was a Lincolnshire man, east coast and there's one little piece I want to recite 'cos I can remember it, which gives you the east coast. 'As when the crest of some slow arching wave, heard at midnight upon that table shore drops flat. And after the great waters break, whitening for half a league, and thin themselves far over sands, marbled with moon and cloud, from less and less to nothing.'

I didn't tell the artistes I was going to put that little bit in. And it was you who brought it out in me.

But now Tennyson's love was for Cambridge, where he was brought up at Trinity.

In Memoriam
ALFRED, LORD TENNYSON

I past beside the reverend walls
    In which of old I wore the gown;
    I roved at random thro' the town,
And saw the tumult of the halls;

And heard once more in college fanes
    The storm their high-built organs make,
    And thunder-music, rolling, shake
The prophet blazon'd on the panes;

And caught once more the distant shout,
    The measured pulse of racing oars
    Among the willows; paced the shores
And many a bridge, and all about

The same gray flats again, and felt
  The same, but not the same; and last
  Up that long walk of limes I past
To see the rooms in which he dwelt.

It was in Trinity College, Cambridge, that Housman, the poet, was a Fellow. He's said to have started a speech there in Trinity Hall with these words: 'In this hall Wordsworth was once drunk and Fawson – that was a very famous scholar – was once sober. A better poet than Fawson, a better scholar than Wordsworth, I stand before you today betwixt and between.'

I love that; it's a very typical piece of Cambridge pedantry. The other side of Housman comes out in his poems, particularly in their 1890 melancholy and sound of words.

Here is Housman at his most summery and luxuriant.

A Shropshire Lad
A. E. HOUSEMAN

On the idle hill of summer,
  Sleepy with the flow of streams,
Far I hear the steady drummer
  Drumming like a noise in dreams.

Far and near and low and louder
  On the roads of earth go by,
Dear to friends and food for powder,
  Soldiers marching, all to die.

By Jove! You can't forget Housman, his power, also his use of words and of the sound of chimes and bells in this extraordinary piece – and I may say Housman was never hanged.

Eight O' Clock
A. E. HOUSEMAN

He stood, and heard the steeple
  Sprinkle the quarters on the morning town.
One, two, three, four, to market-place and people
  It tossed them down.

43

Strapped, noosed, nighing his hour,
    He stood and counted them and cursed his luck;
And then the clock collected in the tower
    Its strength, and struck.

The next piece is by, Eric Walter White, a Bristolian-born poet, who lived latterly in Islington. It's about the death of his wife, Dodo.

The Thirty-Ninth Rose

ERIC WALTER WHITE
In Memoriam Edith Dorothy White (Dodo)
16 October 1909 – 1 July 1977

Thirty-nine roses for thirty-nine summers.
The first summer started late;
The last one was broken . . .

When we knew you had only five months –
Or was it six or seven? – to live,
How the days went scurrying by!
No one could tell what the next day would bring.
When I saw you look in the mirror,
I wondered if you were thinking
Is this the last time I shall look
In this mirror to do my hair
And renew my make-up?
When I saw you climb with increasing difficulty
The stairs from the hall to the floor above,
I wondered if you were thinking
Is this the last time I shall have strength enough
To climb this staircase to go to bed?
When I sat by your bedside and saw
Your eyes open and recognise me,
I wondered if you were thinking
Is this the last time I shall see his features?
But I tried to conceal these thoughts from you
Lest my eyes betray me;
And when the moment came,
It was Sarah who saw you for the last time still alive.
And I who saw you for the first time dead.

I remember how courageously
You fought with the dark angel during those last weeks –
How beneath the sheet your limbs thrashed out,
Trying to ward off the incarcerating mesh
Of the iron maiden of cancer.
It was as if under the implacable glare of ringside lights
Your agony was featured
In a canvas by Francis Bacon.
Who that saw them can forget your agonies? –
The agony of being shifted on to a new pile of pillows:
The agony of the new position:
The agony of the parched tongue;
The agonies from which there seemed to be
No deliverance except through drugs.
And yet there were still occasions when you found
The right touch at the right moment 'marvellous'.

You always hated the voyeur;
But in this succesion of agonies
I found I could not keep away from your bedroom,
I could not, not look at what was happening.
But so as not to disturb you with my glance
I would stand outside the room
And peep through the crack between door and jamb.
Forgive me!
How far have you travelled
Since I entered your bedroom a short while ago
And saw you had just died?
The shadow of this eclipse had already spread over your
    features.
And your skin had the beauty of a waxen mask.
My first thought was that you had stopped
While Sarah and I continued to live.
But later I saw that it was we who had stopped
While you were bound on an unknown voyage
Towards an uncharted goal.
. . . The petals from the thirty-ninth rose
Have fallen upon your shroud;
And now the long loneliness begins.

45

Thank Goodness that there's such good language written and that we've got poets today who can move us deeply.

Readers: Richard Briers, Eleanor Bron

Full Selection:
19th Century Railway Carriages, HAMILTON ELLIS
Isaac Watts' Divine and Moral Songs
The Diary of a Nobody, GEORGE and WEEDON GROSSMITH
Vitae Summa Brevis Spem Nos Vetat Incohare Longam, ERNEST DOWSON
Her Second Husband Hears Her Story, THOMAS HARDY
In Memoriam, ALFRED, LORD TENNYSON
A Shropshire Lad, A. E. HOUSMAN
Eight O'Clock, A.E. HOUSMAN
Pain, ELIZABETH JENNINGS
The Thirty-Ninth Rose, ERIC WALTER WHITE
The Trees, PHILIP LARKIN
Meditation on The A 30, JOHN BETJEMAN
Mr Sponge's Sporting Tour, ROBERT SURTEES
In a Little Wadi, MICHAEL DUGDALE
Christmas JOHN BETJEMAN

SIR LAWRENCE BRAGG

1970

It is a commonplace, I suppose, that whilst there may be many engineers who play the violin, there are few violinists who have any notion of how to build a bridge. Certainly it is true that the majority of people who work in the arts, myself included, have only the haziest knowledge of matters technical and scientific. Nevertheless, this distinguished scientist obviously felt a need to take note of criticism from that quarter: 'It is very well known to our arts colleagues, who never cease to remind us about it, that (a) scientists have hardly any human or artistic feelings at all and (b) that they are quite inarticulate, quite helpless at explaining even such feelings as they have.' However, he did not have the slightest difficulty in including items by Robert Browning, Jane Austen, Sir Arthur Conan Doyle, E. M. Forster, Virginia Woolf and Tolstoy amongst those which had given him great pleasure. Nevertheless, perhaps in order to redress the balance, I have chosen from his programme pieces by two scientists, the second of whom, though, is generally reckoned to be the province of students of English Literature rather than that of budding physicists.

The art of lecturing, of talking about science, has always fascinated me, and Faraday was a great exponent of it. As well as being a very great scientist, probably our greatest scientist since Newton, he was well-known for his talks. His biographer, Bence Jones, said of him: 'His manner was so natural that the thought of any art in his lecturing never occurred to anyone'. Yet these notes show how intensely he studied this art.

Advice to a Lecturer
MICHAEL FARADAY

A lecturer should appear easy and collected, undaunted and unconcerned, his thoughts about him and his mind clear for the contemplation and description of his subject. His action should be slow, easy and natural, consisting principally in changes in the posture of the body, in order to avoid the air of stiffness or sameness that would be otherwise unavoidable.

His whole behaviour should evince a respect for his audience, and he should in no case forget that he is in their presence.

Some lecturers choose to express their thoughts extemporaneously immediately as they should occur to the mind, whilst others previously arrange them and draw them forth on paper.

But although I allow a lecturer to write out his matter, I do *not* approve of his reading it – at least, not as he would a quotation or extract. He should deliver it in a ready and free manner, referring to his book merely as he would to copious notes, and not confining his tongue to the path there delineated but digress as the circumstances may demand or localities allow.

A lecturer falls deeply beneath the dignity of his character when he descends so low as to angle for claps and ask for commendation. Yet I have even seen a lecturer at this point.

I have heard him causelessly condemn his own powers. I have heard him dwell for a length of time on the extreme care and niceness that the experiment he will make requires.

I have heard him hope for indulgence when no indulgence was wanted, and I have heard him declare that the experiment cannot fail from its beauty, its correctness and its application, to gain the approbation of all.

I feel this last is perhaps a little too hard, and I haven't quite got a clear conscience about it. I'm not sure I haven't sometimes angled for claps and commendations. But the main reason for my including those notes is that I think they reveal something of Faraday's greatness.

And now as a scientist I must choose for you something from a scientific paper. The author is explaining how to make a scientific instrument – a sort of large protractor, with scales around the edge and strings going from pins near the middle. And the purpose of it is to find the position of the planets and sun and moon in the sky at any given date. This is how he starts:

In the name of the god pitos & merciable the largere pt thow makest this instrument/ the largere ben thi chef deuisions/ the largere pt ben tho deuisions/ in hem may ben mo smale fraccions/ 'euere the mo of smale fraccions the ner the trowthe of thy conclusions/ tak ther fore a plate of metal or elles a board pt be smothe shaue/ by leuel/ & euene polised of which whan it is rownd (by compas)/ the hole diametre shal contene .72. large enches or elles .6. fote of mesure/ the whiche rownd bord fot it shal nat werpe ne Krooke/the eggs of (the) circumference shal be bownde wt a plate of yren in maner of a karte whel./ this bord yif the likith may be vernissed or elles glewed wt perchemyn for honestyte tak thanne a cercle of metal pt be .2. enche of brede/ this cercle wole I clepe the lymbe of myn equatorie pt was compowned the yer of crist .1932. complet the laste meridie of decembre.

That treatise was apparently never published, that is to say, copied by professional scribes, because of course there was no printing at that time. It is a draft, obviously in the author's own handwriting, with his corrections and emendations written all over it. Now the story about it is as follows: When I was at the Cavendish, I had a young man, a historian of science, Derek Price, working for me on the Cavendish archives; there's a wonderful lot of letters from various professors there. He was working on the letters of our first professor, Clerk Maxwell, and he was in Peterhouse library, where he was getting a lot of his information. He asked the librarian at Peterhouse library whether he had any old scientific documents, just on spec. as it were. The librarian turned up one which had been in the library for about three hundred years. It was ascribed in the catalogue to a man called Bredon.

Now Price knew enough about the history of science to know that Bredon had been dead for a long time in 1392, which was the date of this document. He read it, got more and more suspicious – the book had been bound with big leather thongs sometime in the Middle Ages, and he asked for leave to unbind the thongs because they covered up the margins. In the margins he found what was pretty obviously the name of the author, Chaucer – Geoffrey Chaucer of the Canterbury Tales.

He checked this by going up to the record office where they have the files where Chaucer was a kind of Civil Servant. They said that they had so many files that it would take far too long to go through them all. Price said that he knew the writing so well and that if they would only let him flip through them he would recognise it. To cut a long story short, one appeared and he said, 'I think this looks like it'. They opened it and it was an authorisation for someone to act in Chaucer's place in an office while Chaucer was absent on a mission in France, signed 'Chaucer' – with the signature absolutely identical with the one in the manuscript. So it's pretty well clinched – it's all right.

Chaucer was an excellent amateur astronomer. He wrote a book called *The Astrolabe* and in it he promised another book on the planets. This must be the draft for it which never appeared in print. Chaucer never finished it or corrected it before his death.

My pleasure in this treatise is partly, I'm afraid, an ignoble one. I can't help chortling a little that it should be left to a scientist to discover the only known manuscript in Chaucer's handwriting. Just think of the excitement if he'd discovered another draft for an unpublished Canterbury Tale. But as well as that I think I have a more creditable pleasure in it – the fascination of seeing how six hundred years ago the scientific author set forth his ideas in English.

Readers: Hugh Dickson, Olive Gregg

Full Selection:
Advice to a Lecturer, MICHAEL FARADAY
Home Thoughts from Abroad, ROBERT BROWNING
Emma, JANE AUSTEN
How to Make a Scientific Instrument, GEOFFREY CHAUCER
The Hound of the Baskervilles, ARTHUR CONAN DOYLE
Aspects of the Novel, E. M. FORSTER
The Death of the Moth, VIRGINIA WOOLF
Anna Karenina, LEO TOLSTOY

MELVYN BRAGG

1981

The selection of items for a programme like 'With Great Pleasure' inevitably leads in the end to a sort of autobiography. If 'you are what you eat', then clearly, if you are a thinking person, you are also what you read. What you choose to remember defines you further, so it's not surprising that on occasion presenters of the programme reveal more

*about themselves than they sometimes realise. This was not the case, I
think, with this subject. Daunted by the enormous number of books that
he had clearly remembered with affection, he decided to offer an anthology
of writings about the area in which he grew up, Cumbria and the Lake
District.*

After the middle of the eighteenth century, the writers and
illustrators began to pile on to the new stage coaches coming up
from London, bowl along the new turnpike roads and discover
enough interest in what they found here to have their records
printed and published back in London. Before the end of the
century, and before Wordsworth came back to his birthplace,
there were many guides, engravings and prints galore about this
'barren and frightful' place as Defoe had described it. The one-
armed Joseph Budworth was a typical gossipy traveller of his time
– he came for a fortnight and, like all good travellers, he didn't fail
to leave an account of what he ate.

Dinner at Grasmere
JOSEPH BUDWORTH

After as good and well-dressed a dinner, at Robert Newton's, as a
man could wish, we set out to surmount the steep ascent of Helm
Crag; but the dinner was so cheap, I must mention what it
consisted of:

Roast pike, stuffed,
A boiled fowl,
Veal-cutlets and ham,
Beans and bacon,
Cabbage,
Peas and potatoes,
Anchovy sauce,
Parsley and butter,
Plain butter,
Butter and cheese,
Wheat bread and oat cake,
Three cups of preserved gooseberries, with a bowl of rich
cream in the centre;
For two people, at ten-pence a head.

And that, remember, just before they set out to climb the Fell! Budworth, incidentally, unwittingly caused a local tragedy when he praised the beauty of the daughter of an inn-keeper to such effect that tourists and poets made special journeys to come and see her and a bigamist turned up to marry her. Then he abandoned her – and later was hanged in Carlisle Castle.

It's interesting that, at the time, so little had been written over hundreds of years, in detail, about landscape. And people coming here, and people from here, were about to do a great deal to change that. Because William and Dorothy Wordsworth came back to live in Dove Cottage at Grasmere, a few miles from Cockermouth where they'd been born.

William is a mountain of a poet, but I'd like to start with some of his most mysterious and very gentle short verses on Lucy.

Lucy Poems
WILLIAM WORDSWORTH

Strange fits of passion have I known:
And I will dare to tell,
But in a Lover's ear alone,
What once to me befell.

When she I loved looked every day
Fresh as a rose in June,
I to her cottage bent my way,
Beneath an evening-moon.

Upon the moon I fixed my eye,
All over the wide lea;
With quickening pace my horse drew nigh
Those paths so dear to me.

And now we reached the orchard-plot;
And, as we climbed the hill,
The sinking moon to Lucy's cot
Came near, and nearer still.

What fond and wayward thoughts will slide
Into a Lover's head:
'Oh mercy!' to myself I cried,
'If Lucy should be dead!'

She dwelt among the untrodden ways
   Beside the springs of Dove,
A Maid whom there were none to praise
   And very few to love:

A violet by a mossy stone
   Half hidden from the eye!
Fair as a star, when only one
   Is shining in the sky.

She lived unknown, and few could know
   When Lucy ceased to be;
But she is in her grave, and oh,
   The difference to me!

A slumber did my spirit seal;
   I had no human fears;
She seemed a thing that could not feel
   The touch of earthly years.

No motion has she now, no force;
   She neither hears nor sees,
Rolled round in earth's diurnal course
   With rocks and stones and trees!

Whether those poems were directly inspired by his sister, Dorothy, or not, the fact is that from the 1790s until the end of his life Wordsworth was deeply helped by his sister. As he said: 'She gave me eyes, she gave me ears and humble cares and delicate fears.'

She had a passion for the details of nature and of daily life, which very often started off a poem and not infrequently seems to have been almost a first draft. Here she is writing about what became a famous walk.

Daffodils at Gowbarrow Park
DOROTHY WORDSWORTH

Thursday, 15th April 1802

It was a threatening, misty morning, but mild. We set off after dinner from Eusemere. Mrs Clarkson went a short way with us, but turned back. The wind was furious and we thought we must have turned back. We first rested in the large boathouse, then under a furze bush opposite Mr Clarkson's. Saw the plough going in the field. The wind seized our breath. The lake was rough. There was a boat by itself floating in the middle of the bay below Water Millock. When we were in the woods beyond Gowbarrow Park, we saw a few daffodils close to the waterside. We fancied that the lake had floated the seeds ashore and that the little colony had so sprung up. But as we went along there were more and yet more; and, at last, under the boughs of the trees, we saw that there was a long belt of them along the shore, about the breadth of a country turnpike road.

I never saw daffodils so beautiful. They grew among the mossy stones, about and about them. Some rested their heads upon these stones, as on a pillow, for weariness; and the rest tossed and reeled and danced, and seemed as if they verily laughed with the wind that blew upon them over the lake. They looked so gay, ever glancing, ever changing. The wind blew directly over the lake to them. There was here and there a little knot, and a few stragglers higher up; but they were so few as not to disturb the simplicity, unity, and life of that one busy highway.

And here is what Wordsworth himself made of it in a poem that, once upon a time, most school children used to know by heart:

Daffodils
WILLIAM WORDSWORTH

I wandered lonely as a cloud
That floats on high o'er vales and hills,
When all at once I saw a crowd,
A host, of golden daffodils;
Beside the lake, beneath the trees,
Fluttering and dancing in the breeze.

Continuous as the stars that shine
And twinkle on the Milky Way,
They stretched in never-ending line
Along the margin of a bay;
Ten thousand saw I at a glance,
Tossing their heads in sprightly dance.

The waves beside them danced, but they
Out-did the sparkling waves in glee;
A poet could not but be gay,
In such a jocund company:
I gazed – and gazed – but little thought
What wealth the show to me had brought.

For oft, when on my couch I lie
In vacant or in pensive mood,
They flash upon that inward eye
Which is the bliss of solitude;
And then my heart with pleasure fills,
And dances with the daffodils.

John Ruskin, Arthur Ransome and Beatrix Potter are just three of
the many writers whose childhood visits, particularly to the
southern lakes, affected their lives and brought them back here to
live out most of their adult years. Beatrix Potter's diary can be
compared with Dorothy Wordsworth's journals in the richness
and contentment that they both found in such an apparently
circumscribed place and life,

Extract from Windermere 1895
BEATRIX POTTER

Saturday, August 10th

In afternoon went with pony up Troutbeck and put it up at the
Mortal Man, which looks a very nice little inn. Papa and I walked
up Nanny Lane and got over a stile into the heather, sweet and
heavy with honey. There was a thunder haze, no view, but very
peaceful, except that the stone walls were covered with flying-
ants.

There was an old shepherd half way up the side of Troutbeck,
much bent and gesticulating with a stick. He watched the collie
scouring round over stone walls, coming close past us without
taking the slightest notice. Four or five sheep louped over a wall
at least three feet high, on our right, and escaped the dog's
observation, whereupon the ancient shepherd – a mere speck
in the slanting sunlight down the great hillside, this aged
Wordsworthian worthy – awoke the echoes with a flood of the
most singularly bad language. He gesticulated and the dog ran

round on the top of the dykes, and some young cattle ran down with their tails in the air. We passed him sitting on a wall as we came down, a pleasant, smiling old fellow. We asked him which was Ill Bell, and he leant over the wall – 'ye'll perceive I'm rather hard of hearing' – then we heard that the prize pup at Kelso Show was named 'Sandy Walker'.

Readers: Joan Bakewell, Ronald Herdman.

Full Selection:
Barren and Frightful, DANIEL DEFOE (From A Tour Through the Whole Island of Great Britain)
Dinner at Grasmere, JOSEPH BUDWORTH (From 'A Fortnight's Ramble to the Lakes' Third Edition, 1810)
Mountains as Picturesque Objects, WILLIAM GILPIN (From Observations Relative Chiefly to Picturesque Beauty in the Mountains and Lakes of Cumberland and Westmorland)
Lucy Poems, WILLIAM WORDSWORTH
Daffodils at Cowbarrow Park, DOROTHY WORDSWORTH (From Grasmere Journal)
Daffodils, WILLIAM WORDSWORTH
Trance and Delight, SAMUEL TAYLOR COLERIDGE
Light and Shade at Grasmere and Rydale, DOROTHY WORDSWORTH (From Grasmere Journal)
Meeting with Wordsworth, THOMAS DE QUINCEY
A Merry Meet, JOHN KEATS (From The Life and Letters of John Keats by Lord Houghton)
The Lazy Tour of Two Idle Apprentices, CHARLES DICKENS (From The Wilds of Carrock)
How They Lived at Wastdale Head, HARRIET MARTINEAU (From A Complete Guide to the English Lakes)
Some Celebrated Wrestlers, WILLIAM LITT (From Wrestliana)
D'Ye Ken John Peel, JOHN GRAVES
It's Nobbut Me, JOHN RICHARDSON
Windermere 1895, BEATRIX POTTER
Like a Little Doll, ELIZABETH A. M. ROBERTS and 'MRS N. O. 4'
Sea to the West, NORMAN NICHOLSON
Intimations of Immortality from Recollections of Early Childhood, WILLIAM WORDSWORTH

JAMES CAMERON

1975

James Cameron was a familiar figure in the sixth floor corridors of Broadcasting House whence he visited the office of whichever Archive Features Department producer was working with him at the time on a series of beautifully presented programmes for which the archive material was often merely the peg to enable him to continue to debate his view of the world. A lifetime spent as a journalist had left him not cynical but wise and warm, shot through with a sometimes acerbic common sense. I remember sitting with him on a canal-boat moving slowly past the Snowdon bird house at London Zoo. He was talking into camera – it was some television producer's idea of the perfect setting for Cameron to expound on the joys of the coming week on BBC1. Admiring the grace with which he carried out this trivial task and seeing his frail form set against the colourful, rare birds, it was easy to wonder which in fact was the endangered species.

I don't know why I became so obsessed with the Elizabethans. Of course I do know why: they were meat and drink to any young man trying to learn the riches and resources of the English language, who jumped into the deep end, at the period when they weren't ashamed to be sentimental, and romantic, and even baroque. Though it's still a bit of a mystery to me how that particular sixteenth century produced such a fantastic flowering, how so many marvellous people were writing marvellous things all, as it were, at the same time. Lots of people think I am pretty square about my idolatry of John Donne, for example, but I am besotted by him. When I first came to London I lived in a sort of chambers that were alleged to have been the attics of his house – you know that John Donne was Vicar of Lincoln's Inn. All I knew then was that it was very handy for Fleet Street. But my John Donne kick has lasted forty years. The first present my wife ever gave me was a splendid, expensive Nonesuch Edition of Donne. It was very perceptive, since my own one had broken its back years before.

'Now that thou hast lov'd me one whole day,
Tomorrow when thou leav'st, what wilt thou say?
Wilt thou then antedate some new-made vow?
Or say that now
We are not just those persons which we were?
Or that oaths made in reverential fear
Of love, and his wrath, any may forswear?
Vain lunatic, against these scapes I could
Dispute, and conquer, if I would;
Which I abstain to do,
For by tomorrow, I may think so too.'

He really was a hell of an old Vicar, this John Donne, a real old Reverend Rake. Nevertheless he left something that I think is one of the most tremendous love poems in the world.

'When I died last – and dear, I die
As often as from thee I go,
Though it be but an hour ago,
And Lovers' hours be full of eternity,
I can remember yet, that I
Something did say, and something did bestow;
Though I be dead, which sent me, I should be
Mine own executor and legacy.

I heard me say, Tell her anon,
That my self (that is you, not I)
Did kill me, and when I felt me die,
I bid me send my heart, when I was gone;
But I alas could find there none,

When I had ripp'd me, and search'd where hearts did lie;
It killed me again, that I who still was true,
In life, in my last Will should cozen you.

Yet I found something like a heart,
But colours it and corners had,
It was not good, it was not bad,
It was entire to none, and few had part.
As good as could be made by art
It seem'd; and therefore for our losses sad
I meant to send this heart insead of mine.
But oh, no man could hold it, for 'twas thine.'

Possibly because I work in a context so different, so much coarser and more hasty and immediate, these sixteenth century cadences fill me with such nourishment and love and envy.

I like the anonymous poets of the Bible as much as I dislike, shall I say, Hymns Ancient and Modern. Obviously an enormous volume of poetry has come out of the need of man to come to terms with the supernatural, the Creator, religion, whatever it may be – not necessarily Christian; look at the vast epic poetry of the Hindus or the Hebrews – presumably because when he was faced with a problem like that, man felt he had to adopt a special literary formula, and it came out as poetry. Naturally. For me, I'm obliged to say, when it's theological it's beyond me and when it's pietistic I leave it alone. A very few men have been accepted and embraced by both the Church and the poets, and I would suggest that by far and away the most sincere and interesting of these is Gerard Manley Hopkins, who became a Jesuit in the last century. I don't know whether many people read Hopkins now but for a very long time he, more than most poets, was examined and analysed and argued about, not so much for his religious content (which was agonisingly deep) but for his poetic *technicalities*, the elaborations of his word-patterns, his craftsman's innovations, the so-called 'sprung rhythms' and so on. He was a great questioner of everything, from religious dogma to traditional verse forms. Even as a small schoolboy in Highgate he could write a very cheeky little couplet: 'A little sickness in the air, From too much fragrance everywhere.'

Some people have hinted that Hopkins was a poet despite his priesthood. I simply wouldn't know, but I do know that for years and years I've carried in my head one verse of his, written as a priest who trusts his God, but can still argue with him – *Justus quidem tu es, Domine, si disputem tecem . . .*

Thou Art Indeed Just, Lord
GERARD MANLEY HOPKINS

Thou art indeed just, Lord, if I contend
With thee; but, Sir, so what I plead is just.
Why do sinners' ways prosper? and why must
Disappointment all I endeavour end?

Were thou my enemy, O thou my friend,
How would'st thou worse, I wonder, than thou dost
Defeat, thwart me? Oh, the sots and thralls of lust
Do in spare hours more thrive than I that spend,

Sir, life upon thy cause. See, banks and brakes
Now, leavèd how thick! lacèd they are again
With fretty chervil; look, and fresh wind shakes

Them; birds build – but not I build; no, but strain
Time's eunuch, and not breed one work that wakes.
Mine, O thou lord of life, send my roots rain.

What writer in the world hasn't known the agony of that dilemma? Surely only one poet has ever confessed that he had dried up, and expressed it in words that showed, so abundantly, that he hadn't – a pretty serious lesson for any writer, great or little. Though not an easy one to learn.

Readers: Clive Merrison, Margaret Robertson, John Samson

Full Selection:
Defence of Poesie, SIR PHILIP SYDNEY
Now That Thou Hast Lov'd Me, JOHN DONNE
When I Died Last, JOHN DONNE
The Merchant of Venice, Act V, WILLIAM SHAKESPEARE
Essay on Wilfred Owen, DYLAN THOMAS
Exposure, WILFRED OWEN
It Seemed That Out of Battle I Escaped, WILFRED OWEN

CHARLES CAUSLEY

1977

*At the time of writing, Charles Causley had just been awarded the CBE.
Let us hope that it is merely the first step to greater honours for this fine
poet and Cornishman. A sense of pride in his origins permeated the
programme, not a sense of place and people only, but a feel for myth, the
idea that every stone could and does tell a story, a story simple enough for
children, which somehow contains a hook into the darker recesses of adult
consciousness.*

It was Noel Coward who remarked on the potency of what he
called cheap music, and for those of us who go through life as
book worms – or as a book anaconda in my case – I think the same
is true of literature. The sort of reading that's given me the
greatest pleasure, the most lasting blow to the senses, isn't

necessarily a spectacularly fine piece of writing by a great writer. A lot depends on who we were, and even where we were, when we first read it.

The very first poem I remember hearing at my primary school I've always thought a masterpiece, and dearly wish I'd written it myself. It's a murder ballad; author: anon. I should also tell you that I was madly in love with the infant teacher who read it to us. I can see her now: tall, calm amid the smells and squalls of the baby class; a pre-Raphaelite beauty, with cool, marble hands and soft brown hair hanging below her shoulders.

As for the poem itself, I had no idea that – in varying European forms – it perhaps had its origins in Scandinavian myth and the death of Balder, the god of light, or that it's believed by some to be an allegorical account of the murder of William Rufus in the New Forest in the year 1100, as well as – a bit nearer our own time – an ironic tale of the end of the career, in the eighteenth century, of Sir Robert Walpole.

I enjoyed – and enjoy – the poem as a poem about the death of that bold and independent bird the robin.

One little point about the verse:

> Who'll toll the bell?
> I said the Bull,
> Because I can pull . . .

How often have you seen him depicted as a farmyard bull, of massive animal architecture? I'm certain we should really see a bird here, the bullfinch, for all the other creatures in the poem are small ones: sparrow, beetle, fly, fish, linnet and so on.

Who Killed Cock Robin

Who killed Cock Robin?
I, said the sparrow,
With my bow and arrow,
I killed Cock Robin.

Who saw him die?
I, said the Fly,
With my little eye,
I saw him die.

Who caught his blood?
I, said the Fish,
With my little dish,
I caught his blood.

Who'll make the shroud?
I, said the Beetle,
With my thread and needle,
I'll make the shroud.

Who'll dig his grave?
I, said the Owl,
With my pick and shovel,
I'll dig his grave.

Who'll be the parson?
I, said the Rook,
With my little book,
I'll be the parson.

Who'll be the clerk?
I, said the Lark,
If it's not in the dark,
I'll be the clerk.

Who'll carry the link?
I, said the Linnet,
I'll fetch it in a minute,
I'll carry the link.

Who'll be chief mourner?
I, said the Dove,
I mourn for my love,
I'll be chief mourner.

Who'll carry the coffin?
I, said the Kite,
If it's not through the night,
I'll carry the coffin.

Who'll bear the pall?
We, said the Wren,
Both the cock and the hen,
We'll bear the pall.

Who'll sing the psalm?
I, said the Thrush,
As she sat on a bush,
I'll sing a psalm.

Who'll toll the bell?
I, said the Bull,
Because I can pull,
I'll toll the bell.

All the birds of the air
Fell a-sighing and a-sobbing,
When they heard the bell toll
For poor Cock Robin.

Poor Cock Robin. How skilfully that anonymous author calls forth our sympathy for the fabled bird that was believed to spread leaves over not only the Babes in the Wood, but over all lost and dead travellers! An animal poem I didn't hear at school – though if I had, I know I'd have loved it – was written by a Cornish poet who was also a Cornish miner. John Harris was born the eldest of ten children, at Six Chimneys Cottage in Camborne, in the year 1820. His father was a miner and small farmer, and at the age of ten John was put to work dressing copper ore at the giant Dolcoath mine. By the time he was twelve years old, he was working underground. He continued as a miner for a quarter of a century more, at a time when the average age of miners at death in many parts of Cornwall ranged from twenty to thirty.

John Harris was a compulsive writer, quite undeterred by poverty. If he hadn't got any paper, he wrote his poems on tiles and roof-slates, on his fingernails, on iron wedges in the mine, even inside his hat. When he ran out of ink, he made his own out of blackberry juice. The poem I've chosen is a piercingly sharp, as well as infinitely tender evocation of a childhood experience I'm sure almost everyone shares: the funeral of a little creature who was not only a valuable working member of a poor family of those days, a provider of food for the pot, but also a dearly loved pet – in this case, a ferret. The actors in this drama of the last rites are all children.

The Burial
JOHN HARRIS

Will's ferret was buried this morn:
    When Samuel came down from his bed,
He whisper'd, with aspect forlorn,
    'O Kitty, Will's ferret is dead.'

And Kitty soon told it to Mark,
    And Mark to the rest of his clan
We sorrow'd with visages dark,
    As if we were mourning a man.

'Come, Ann, let us lay her to rest,
    And you must prepare us a bier:
We will heap the cold earth on her breast,'
    And we wiped from our eyelids a tear.

So Ann made a coffin so small,
    Of cast-off brown paper and thread:
This served for a shroud and a pall, –
    False trappings, unknown to the dead.

And Samuel was sexton and clerk,
    And Benjamin bearer so brave,
While Kitty, and Jacob, and Mark
    Soon bore her away to the grave.

My mother was curious enow,
    And so she came softly behind,
Well pleased with her children, I trow,
    Who to the poor brute were so kind.

'Neath the hawthorn its grave was dug deep,
    With sharp-pointed pickaxe and spade,
Lie down, little ferret, and sleep
    On the couch that affection has made.

At the age of thirty-seven, Harris was rescued from a life of labour in the mines to become a kind of itinerant scripture-reader, and he went on to produce fifteen or sixteen collections of verse altogether.

The poet Percy Bysshe Shelley was drowned at the age of thirty while sailing in the Italian Gulf of Spezia in the summer of 1822. He had, no doubt still has, many detractors, both as a poet and a person. But his friend, the Cornishman Edward John Trelawney once said, significantly, 'To know an author personally is too often but to destroy the illusion created by his works . . .' and that, 'Shelley was a grand exception to this rule'. And Lord Byron called him 'the best and most benevolent of men; they hooted him out of his country like a mad dog, for questioning a dogma.'

My feelings about that sweet natured, unselfish, immensely courageous poet are by no means all sad ones. One of his earliest – and one of his best – biographers was Thomas Jefferson Hogg: the friend and exact contemporary – he was born in 1792 – who was sent down from Oxford after the furore created by the publication of the poet's famous pamphlet called 'The Necessity of Atheism'. Like Edward John Trelawney, Hogg produces a marvellously vivid portrait of Shelley. Here, for instance, is the poet with his books, and, a little later, being pursued by another poet, Robert Southey, who wants to read his latest work to him. Shelley, at this time, is aged twenty and living in Keswick in Cumberland.

Shelley at Home
THOMAS JEFFERSON HOGG

Shelley . . . was always reading; at his meals a book lay by his side, on the table, open. Tea and toast were often neglected, his author seldom; his mutton and potatoes might grow cold; his interest in a work never cooled. He invariably sallied forth, book in hand, reading to himself, if he was alone; if he had a companion, reading aloud. He took a volume to bed with him, and read as long as his candle lasted; he then slept – impatiently no doubt – until it was light, and he recommenced reading at the early dawn . . . In consequence of this great watching, and of almost incessant reading, he would often fall asleep in the daytime – dropping off in a moment – like an infant. He often quietly transferred himself from his chair to the floor, and slept soundly on the carpet, and in the winter upon the rug, basking in the warmth like a cat, and like a cat his little round head was roasted before a blazing fire. If anyone humanely covered the poor head to shield it from the heat, the covering was impatiently put aside in his sleep . . .

Southey was addicted to reading his terrible epics – before they were printed – to anyone who seemed to be a fit subject for the cruel experiment. He soon set his eyes on the newcomer, and one day having effected the capture of Shelley, he immediately lodged him securely in a little study upstairs, carefully locking the door upon himself and his prisoner and putting the key in his waistcoat pocket. There was a window in the room it is true, but it was so high above the ground that Baron Trenck himself would not have attempted it.

'Now you shall be delighted,' Southey said: 'but sit down.'

Poor Bysshe sighed, and took his seat at the table. The author seated himself opposite, and placing his MS on the table, before him, began to read slowly and distinctly. The poem, if I mistake not, was 'The Curse of Kehama'. Charmed with his own composition the admiring author read on, varying his voice occasionally, to point out the finer passages and invite applause. There was no commendation; no criticism; all was hushed. This was strange. Southey raised his eyes from the neatly written MS: Shelley had disappeared. This was still more strange. Escape was impossible; every precaution had been taken, yet he had vanished. Shelley had glided noiselessly from his chair to the floor, and the insensible young Vandal lay buried in profound sleep underneath the table.

Readers: William Squire, Margot van der Burgh

Full Selection:
Cock Robin trad
The Burial, JOHN HARRIS
Reticent, D. M. THOMAS
A Cornish Anthology. Billy Bray: Miner, Evangelist, ed. A. L. ROWSE
After Billy Bray, JACK CLEMO
The Aboriginals, RONALD TAMPLIN
The Unicorn in the Garden, JAMES THURBER
Shelley at Home, THOMAS JEFFERSON HOGG
Ozymandias, P. B. SHELLEY

Mrs Malone, ELEANOR FARJEON
Framed in a First-Storey Winder anon from 'Strange to Tell' ed.
D. SAUNDERS

PROFESSOR ANTHONY CLARE

1985

The rehearsal had finished early and everybody involved had a couple of hours to kill. This can sometimes be a difficult time, with the discovery that whilst the members of the group may be perfectly friendly and amiably disposed towards one another, they actually have very little in common other than the purpose for which they were assembled. Under such circumstances conversation is frequently desultory, books are produced, one person takes a walk, another phones his agent until suddenly it's time for the recording, the audience is appreciative, it's gone well and in the euphoria that follows we all get on swimmingly and exchange telephone numbers. That wasn't the case on this occasion. The conversation flowed in that two hours. It became clear that the interviewing style Anthony Clare employs for 'In the Psychiatrist's Chair' isn't solely a professional technique, but arises from his genuine interest and concern for people and their well-being. A man of gentle humour, he confessed 'I became almost suicidal in my search for a selection that makes me laugh. It was the surfeit not the shortage that almost killed me.' In the end he settled on Tom Sharpe 'partly because I still remember my father-in-law being rendered speechless with laughter one Christmas reading "Wilt".' For the rest, included in his immaculately written script, aside from Joyce and Yeats, perhaps predictable choices from an Irishman, were pieces which reflected his professional, and therefore humanitarian, concerns. At the end of the evening he drove everybody home.

Faced with the near-impossibility of selecting pieces for this programme, I have chosen pieces of prose and poetry which, in addition to giving me pleasure and provocation, are in some way linked with elements in my own life, usually people. My own love for and interest in literature are due, in great part, to my wife who is better read and certainly far more literate than I can ever hope to be, and a Jesuit teacher at my day school in Dublin, a hater of set texts and smelly orthodoxies who struggled manfully to introduce a scruffy gaggle of boys to the glorious repository of English literature. He was not, however, very fond of my next choice despite the fact that the Jesuits educated him too.

I only really discovered what it is like to be a Dubliner when I left Dublin, first to spend a year as a newly-qualified intern in America and later, and more permanently, when I crossed the Irish sea to work in London. My trip to the US was purely pragmatic – I wanted to marry my wife. Irish hospitals, unlike American ones, did not provide married quarters for their junior staff – like the church, they regarded sexual activity, even of the marital and therefore approved sort, as a most regrettable distraction and I suspect that some senior Irish physicians of the time would have shared Freud's view, a man they otherwise abhorred, that much of the good things man gets up to are sublimations of unexpressed sexual needs. To this day I cherish towards the United States the most intense and confused feelings. I am appalled by the brashness and entranced by the energy. It is fashionable for British observers to dismiss America as adolescent, but then there is something geriatric about current British preoccupations with the past and in contrast to the dynamism of New York, London has all the trappings of an admittedly well-appointed museum.

In the 1960s and 1970s, the formative years of my life, termed by Tom Wolfe 'The Purple Decades' there was a revival of charismatic religion, a phenomenon common to Western society but, of course, at its most flamboyant across the Atlantic. For my own part, such little sympathy as I have with charismatic faith is due in part to several summers spent in Assisi in Umbria, a heavenly paradise of a place where not only is Francis buried, but my namesake, St Clare too. Incidentally, did you know that St Clare is the patron saint of television? It is, as you might expect of such matters, a most fitting choice in that once while in her cell at the convent of San Damiano she heard and saw mass underway at the distant church of St Francis of Assisi – the first recorded occurrence of dual transmission and, to date, the only one without elaborate equipment – indeed without any equipment!

Another namesake of whom I am proud – although sadly we are in no way related – is John Clare, the nineteenth century poet. Clare, the son of a poor labourer, wrote some of the most lyrical poetry of his time. He suffered a severe mental breakdown as a young man and spent the rest of his life in a mental hospital. During his stay he wrote an intensely moving poem which to this day remains one of the clearest statements of the enormity that is mental illness and it is for this reason and the fact that it is a lovely creation that I have chosen 'Written in Northampton County Asylum'.

Written in Northampton County Asylum
JOHN CLARE

I am! yet what I am who cares, or knows?
   My friends forsake me like a memory lost.
I am the self-consumer of my woes;
   They rise and vanish, an oblivious host,
Shadows of life, whose very soul is lost,
   And yet I am – I live – though I am toss'd

Into the nothingness of scorn and noise,
   Into the living sea of waking dream,
Where there is neither sense of life, nor joys,
   But the huge shipwreck of my own esteem
And all that's dear. Even those I loved the best
Are strange – nay they are stranger than the rest.

I long for scenes where man has never trod –
   For scenes where women never smiled or wept –
There to abide with my Creator, God,
   And sleep as I in childhood sweetly slept,
Full of high thoughts, unborn. So let me lie, –
The grass below; above, the vaulted sky.

Perhaps it is because I am a doctor but for me the one real unanswerable question is not that of God's existence but suffering's.

70

I try and convince myself of its efficacy, that it cleanses, elevates, exalts and that only he who has suffered is privy to certain truths. Yet I am not convinced and most of the time I regard suffering as a barbarity and the fight to eliminate it the noblest and most worthwhile fight of all. There is now a rich literature on illness and suffering written from the inside as it were. One such creation is 'The Journal of a Disappointed Man and a Last Diary' written by W. N. P. Barbellion, who suffered a particularly malignant form of multiple sclerosis. Like so many sufferers Barbellion was, as his brother wrote, 'as greedy as a shark for life in the raw, for the whole of life' but, understandably, there were moments of intense, despairing gloom, moments captured in the remarkable diary which he kept regularly during the years before his death.

The Journal of a Disappointed Man and a Last Diary
W. N. P. BARBELLION

February 3rd

Suffering does not only insulate. It drops its victim on an island in an ocean desert where he sees men as distant ships passing. I not only feel alone, but very far away from you all. But what is my suffering? Not physical pain. I have none. Pain brings clusters of one's fellows – a toothache is intelligible. But when I say I have grown tired of myself, have outlived myself, am unseasonable and 'mopy' like a doomed swallow in November, it is something that requires a John Galsworthy to understand. The world to me is but a dream or mock show; and we all therein but Pantalones and Anticks to my severe contemplations. This used to be a transitory impression that amused my curiosity. But it hurts and bewilders now that it has become the permanent complexion of my daily existence, when I long for real persons and real things. Tinsel and pictures are melancholy substitutes to anyone heart-hungry for the touch of real hands, and the sound of real voices. Acute mental pain at intervals seizes me with pincers and casts me helpless into the whirlpool – it may be W–'s despair, or the failure to find a home for me to go to. But there are spasms of reality, the momentary opening and closing of a shutter on Life. As soon as they are over, I at once relapse into the dull monotone of misery and picture-show.

I have not left my room since November 11th. I eat well, sleep well, am in possesion of all my higher faculties – those for feeling and thinking. But I can't get out.

I think sometimes folk do not come to see me because I am such a gruesome object. It is not pleasant to feel you are gruesome. I have outstayed my welcome. I know everyone will be relieved to hear of my death – no doubt for my sake, as they will eagerly point out, but also for their sake, as I believe. Yet now and then in selfish and ignoble moods, I, being an egotist, fancy I would like some loving hands to clutch at me, in a blind, ineffectual effort to save me in any condition if only alive.

February 4th
The last part of yesterday's entry was maudlin tosh – 'entirely foreign to my nature'. I hereby cancel it.

I intended to end my selection with Emily Dickinson, a poet who more than once concerned herself with medicine and madness. It was she who wrote:

> Faith is a fine invention
> For gentlemen who see;
> But microscopes are prudent
> In an emergency.

As fine a comment on the limits of belief and the usefulness of science as I know.

But my last choice is – Shakespeare. Having once seen Gielgud as Prospero, it can only be that great speech in which the mystery and abyss of existence is stared in the eye. Before it, an excerpt from a great psychiatrist, the late Sir Aubrey Lewis, one-time director of the Maudsley Hospital, where I trained and spent many happy years. Here is Lewis speculating on the character of Shakespeare.

The Psychology of Shakespeare
AUBREY LEWIS

It may be accepted that in his early manhood, when witty talkers, young lovers and fiery adventurers predominated in his plays, Shakespeare himself was ardent and bold; later when deep and moral problems, the crudities and sufferings that sexuality entails, the humiliations imposed by the imperious body and its desires, the meaning of death, frustration and disillusionment – when these were the central themes of his plays, and the chief characters in them were powerful fathers and rulers who suffered defeat, we may, hesitantly, surmise that Shakespeare had himself an anguished maturity, to be succeeded at last by the relative serenity and renunciation which are expressed in *The Tempest*, his final play. There he had come to the time when he must break his magic staff and drown his book deeper than did ever plummet sound; he asked for solemn music, and he spoke his farewell nobly:

> Our revels now are ended. These our actors
> As I foretold you, were all spirits and
> Are melted into air, into thin air;
> And, like the baseless fabric of this vision,
> The cloud-capp'd towers, the gorgeous palaces,
> The solemn temples, the great globe itself,
> Yea, all which it inherit, shall dissolve,
> And, like this insubstantial pageant faded,
> Leave not a wrack behind. We are such stuff
> As dreams are made on; and our little life
> Is rounded with a sleep.

Readers: Andrew Sachs, Rosalind Shanks

Full Selection:
Journey of the Magi, T. S. ELIOT
The Dead, JAMES JOYCE
The Purple Decades, TOM WOLFE
Written in Northampton County Asylum, JOHN CLARE
The Plague, ALBERT CAMUS
The Second Coming, W. B. YEATS
Wilt, TOM SHARPE
Riders in the Chariot, PATRICK WHITE
The Journal of a Disappointed Man and a Last Diary, W. N. P. BARBELLION

The Psychology of Shakespeare, AUBREY LEWIS
Our Revels now are Ended – from The Tempest, WILLIAM
SHAKESPEARE

RENE CUTFORTH

1970

*Rene Cutforth was a journalist of what is sometimes, wincingly, called
the 'Old School' – a term of approbation generally, it is often used by an
older person to underline the failings of a younger generation whilst being
forgiving of those of the professional under discussion. Not being of
Cutforth's generation, I can offer the opinion that in his case it does not
seem totally unfair. It is rare nowadays to hear the news reported in a way
that employs the English language in anything other than its most
functional expression, as if words were merely nuts and bolts without the
potential of being artists' materials. In fairness the ability to conjure up
pictures in the mind with a clarity and emotional truth that rendered the
invention of television superfluous was one given to few. As a young
studio manager in the 1960s I can remember being faced in the studio with
this, to me, elderly and slightly hungover man possessed of a voice which
was the audible equivalent of malt whisky, and a face which looked as if it
had been preserved in it. Apparently, he had been out of favour and giving
him a small series of four programmes was a first attempt at rehabili-
tation. In charge of the proceedings was Francis 'Jack' Dillon, a distinguished Features producer who managed, well after retirement, to be
barred from the BBC Club for disorderly behaviour! After recording
the first programme, I rushed back to the office and demanded to be
allocated to work on the rest of the series. I had never heard scripts
as good. It wasn't until later that I learned that Cutforth had written
them on rising from Jack's office floor after sleeping off the previous*

night's drinking. Certainly, by far the most substantial part of his edition of 'With Great Pleasure', recorded in the Concert Hall, Broadcasting House, was a paean of praise to a nearby public house.

What I've chosen has, I hope, some bearing on the climate and the situation my friends and I find ourselves in. Particularly since most of them are about my age, with aerials of similar wavelengths and have had something to do with what I must be careful not to call 'the wireless'. But most of all because a great many of them have been through either the full course or the shorter course in Further Education at the George public house in Mortimer Street.

Since the George and its denizens is part of the theme of this programme I'll go on about it a bit. When I first pushed open the George's gloomy swing door in 1946, the interior could be described as austere.

It had, and still has, a good deal of rather overbearing mahogany and mirrors brassily inscribed with the names of forgotten drinks, Shrub for instance, and somebody's Entire, whatever that might mean.

The damp dun-coloured floor could have been made of stone or wood or almost anything, but it was in fact a piece of lino glued to the foundations with beer. There wasn't much light and the effect of the mahogany and the lights refracted through red and yellow bottles was rather like diving into a fruit cake stuffed with cherries and bits of candied peel. You would get mousetrap cheese and onions if you made a fuss but that was all the George had to offer in those days except the company.

It was crammed to bursting with poets and producers and actors in pursuit of the producers, and professors with Third Programme talks, and journalists from the Newsroom and people who described themselves as writers but talked so much in the George they never got round to putting anything down. Many of the members were idiosyncratic to the verge of eccentricity. There was the poet who at a certain stage in the evening rang his own telephone number to see if he was there; the brilliant writer who'd written nothing since the early part of the war and who stood with a silver-knobbed stick in one hand and a cigar in the other and claimed your undivided attention for hour after hour for an endless shouted fantasy about himself. There the professor who's hobby in life was the punctuation of the poems of Pope. He collected the commas particularly. There was a Highland film producer, almost incomprehensible, who forced you by sheer pertinacity to join him in weeping for his poor old father. There were Welshmen in search of harmony and Irishmen in search of injustice.

It was said of the George that more books were conceived there which never came to delivery than in any other place on earth. But it was the poets, scratching and biting, who made the place. Every contemporary poet you'd ever heard of came in at one time or another, but chief of them all in the George in the fifties was Louis MacNeice, good poet, economical of speech, tall and saturnine and brooding over his Guiness.

Poets in those days were apt to give out from time to time a sort of cultural weather forecast, with observations about the prevailing wind and any compass bearings they had to offer. Auden could frighten you to death with a weather report, but no one was better at them then MacNeice. He told you exactly what it was that was rumbling about in a disquieting way at the back of your mind and since I want to remind you of the last great cataclysmic change in the weather which has made so much difference to our lives I am including the very last weather report that Louis MacNeice wrote in 1959, part of the dedication to his book *85 Poems*.

To Hedli from *85 Poems*
LOUIS MACNEICE

Acting younger than I am and thinking older
I have buried so many stray moments in this volume
That I feel shrunk; as though those April answers
Had withered off their Question and now turning,
As the year turns, I bind up ghost and image
To give them, Hedli, to you, a makeshift present.

For having lived, and too much, in the present,
Askance at the coming gods, estranged from those older
Who had created my fathers in their image,

I stand here now dumbfounded by the volume
Of angry sound which pours from every turning
On those who only lately knew the answers.

So I lay my ear to the ground and no one answers
Though I know that the Word, like a bulb, is there, is present
And there the subterranean wheels keep turning
To make the world gush green when, we being older,
Others will be in their prime to drench a volume
In the full leaf of insight and bloom of image.

At one time I was content if things would image
Themselves in their own dazzle, if the answers
Came quick and smooth and the great depth and volume
Of the cold sea would wash me the chance present,
Bone or shell or message from some older
Castaway for whom there was no returning.

But now I am not content, the leaves are turning
And the gilt flaking from each private image
And all the poets I know, both younger and older,
Condemned to silence unless they divine the answers
Which our grim past has buried in our present
And which are no more than groped for in this volume.

Still at this point I tender you this volume
In hopes, my dearest, that your fingers turning
These pages may let fall, among those present,
Some greeting on my waifs and wraiths of image
And half-blind questions that still lack their answers,
Which lack grows no way less as I grow older.

Older and older. Which was the right turning?
Rhythm and image and still at best half answers
And at half volume. But take this; it is a present.

Reader: Hugh Burden

Full Selection:
To Hedli, LOUIS MACNEICE
Cards of Identity, NIGEL DENNIS

To the Unknown Citizen, W. H. AUDEN
The Garden Party, HILAIRE BELLOC
The Love Song of J. Alfred Prufrock, T. S. ELIOT
Part XI of Amours de Voyage, ARTHUR HUGH CLOUGH
Scoop, EVELYN WAUGH
Lord Hippo, HILAIRE BELLOC
How the Kooks Crumble, JAMES THURBER

DAVID DAICHES

1985

It has been a pleasure of mine, over many years, to produce on location in the Scottish border country a number of Features, written and presented by Hugh Douglas, about authors who had had close connections with that part of the world – Robert Burns, John Buchan, James Hogg and Sir Walter Scott. Daiches, a distinguished academic, editor and critic made vivid contributions to the programmes on Hogg and Scott. He must have written and lectured on them many times, but on each occasion, as we sat in his Edinburgh house listening to him talking so ebulliently, it was as if he had just discovered a fresh and exciting new talent. We recorded his edition of 'With Great Pleasure' in Sir Walter Scott's house at Abbotsford, guests of Walter Scott's delightful great-great-great-great-great-grand-daughters, Jean and Patricia Maxwell-Scott. As so often before they made us warmly welcome. They must by now be used to the BBC paraphernalia, but they turned not a hair at the arrival of an audience of about thirty to be squeezed into the library. Many of them were members of Burns' clubs and so on whom Hugh and I had met on previous trips and knew to be jolly and entertaining. And so they were, before and after the recording. During the performance, which they claimed to have enjoyed, they remained largely silent and straight-faced, taking their pleasure seriously. *Nothing wrong with that of course; it's just that it's difficult to convey on tape that they are having a good time when they don't make a sound. And entertaining David's presentation certainly was. All his enthusiasm and joy when talking about his favourite writers would have been clear to the most distant listener at home.*

Let us move to the early eighteenth century, to a poem of melancholy, the elegant pensiveness of Matthew Prior. It's carefully chiselled down as a work of art. It is done with wit and done with a kind of stoical acceptance – life is like this; we civilised men know that people cling to life even after they have got nothing left; they may be poor, they may be ill, they may be better dead, but they cling to life and that is the lesson of history. It's almost as if the poem exists for the sake of the last line, 'Unwilling to retire, tho' weary'. It sums up the human condition as he sees it. The poem is called 'Written in the Beginning of Mezeray's History of France'. I've never read Mezeray's *History of France* and I don't think many people would have remembered it if Matthew Prior hadn't written in the fly-leaf.

Written in the Beginning of Mezeray's History of France
MATTHEW PRIOR

Whate'er thy Countrymen have done,
By law and Wit, by Sword and Gun,
In Thee is faithfully recited:
And all the Living World, that view
Thy Work, give thee the Praises due:
At once Instructed and Delighted.

Yet for the Fame of all these Deeds,
What Beggar in the Invalides,
With Lameness broke, with Blindness smitten,
Wished ever decently to die,
To have been either Mezeray,
Or any Monarch He has written?

It strange, dear Author, yet it true is,
That down from Pharamond to Louis,
All covet Life, yet call it Pain;

All feel the Ill, yet shun the Cure:
Can Sense this Paradox endure?
Resolve me, Cambray or Fontaine.

The Man in graver Tragic known,
Tho' his best Part long since was done,
Still on the Stage desires to tarry:
And He who play'd the Harlequin,
After the Jest still loads the Scene,
Unwilling to retire, tho' weary.

Dr Johnson I think is the greatest epistolary in the history of literature. This is his letter to Lord Chesterfield. Lord Chesterfield had been asked by Johnson – or at least he'd tried to ask him but he didn't get any contact with him – to help him when he was working on his great dictionary. He didn't, but after the dictionary was finally completed after many years of solitary labour Chesterfield wrote two articles in a periodical, known as *The World*, praising it. And Johnson felt it was a bit belated.

This letter is generally taken to have marked the end of the age of patronage, the subsidising of literature by men of power and money to whom authors had to be subservient. Johnson put an end to that with a bang.

Boswell's Johnson

To the Right Honourable The Earl of Chesterfield. February 7, 1755.

My Lord,
I have lately been informed, by the proprietor of *The World*, that two papers, in which my Dictionary is recommended to the public, were written by your lordship. To be so distinguished is an honour, which being very little accustomed to favours from the great, I know not well how to receive, or in what terms to acknowledge.

When, upon some slight encouragement, I first visited your lordship, I was overpowered, like the rest of mankind, by the enchantment of your address, and could not forbear to wish that I must boast myself *Le vainqueur du vainqueur de la torte*: that I might obtain that regard for which I saw the world contending; but I found my attendance so little encouraged, that neither pride nor modesty would suffer me to continue it. When I had once addressed your lordship in public, I had exhausted all the art of pleasing which a retired and uncourtly scholar can possess. I had done all that I could; and no man is well pleased to have his all neglected, be it ever so little.

Seven years, my lord, have now passed since I waited in your outward rooms, or was repulsed from your door; during which time I have been pushing my work through difficulties, of which it is useless to complain, and have brought it, at last, to the verge of publication, without one act of assistance, one word of encouragement, or one smile of favour. Such treatment I did not expect, for I never had a patron before.

The shepherd in *Virgil* grew at last acquainted with Love, and found him a native of the rocks.

Is not a patron, my lord, one who looks with unconcern on a man struggling for life in the water, and, when he has reached ground, encumbers him with help? The notice which you have been pleased to take of my labours, had it been early, had been kind; but it has been delayed till I am indifferent, and cannot enjoy it; till I am solitary and cannot impart it; till I am known and do not want it. I hope it is no very cynical asperity not to confess obligations where no benefit has been received, or to be unwilling that the public should consider me as owing that to a patron which Providence has enabled me to do for myself. Having carried on my work thus far with so little obligation to any favourer of learning. I shall not be disappointed though I shall conclude it, if less be possible, with less; for I have been long wakened from that dream of hope, in which I once boasted myself with so much exultation.

My Lord, your lordship's most humble,
Most obedient servant,
Sam Johnson.

Terrific stuff. Johnson's wife had died while he was writing the dictionary hence that extraordinary three-fold thing: 'till I am indifferent, and cannot enjoy it; till I am solitary, and cannot impart it; till I am known and do not want it'. The way he spits that out! And the way he avoids having to sign himself 'your lordship's obedient servant': The time has long since passed 'in which I once boasted myself with so much exultation . . .', so he even gets out of the conventional compliment at the end.

And now I turn to something very different, an extract from Robert Louis Stevenson's unfinished masterpiece – he died in the middle of it – *Weir of Hermiston*. It is the book in which the father–son conflict which was so strong in all Stevenson's feelings and writings is most perfectly achieved in fiction. He had a great conflict with his own father whom he both dearly loved and bitterly quarrelled with on matters of religion. And again and again in his novels, in his letters, in his essays you get reflections of this, but he finally found the appropriate literary way of purging himself of this in the situation in *Weir of Hermiston*, in the relationship between the father, the tough judge – Scots speaking, he'd have nothing to do with the new-fangled English modes of speech – the old, traditional, stern, cruel, but just Scottish judge and his sensitive son of a sensitive and weak mother. Strong in his own way, but very differently from his father, the son in this conflict, in this dialogue, speaks English. The father speaks good old-fashioned Scots as they did so often on the bench in those days, at the very end of the eighteenth century. What happens is this Weir of Hermiston, the judge, the justice clerk, had sentenced to death a man called Duncan Jopp for sheep-stealing which was then a capital offence. The son, Archie, had been present at the court and was absolutely horrified at what he considered to be the glee with which his father hunted down this wretched man. And that evening at the Speculative Society, in Edinburgh, at the debate he opposed capital punishment, his mind full of the horror of his father's sentencing this wretched man to death. And then when he was publicly hanged shortly afterwards, he attended the hanging and was absolutely revolted. He cried out against what was happening even though he knew his father was responsible for it. When he gets home he finds that his father had heard about what he had done and this is an abridged version of the interview that takes place. The father speaking Scots, the son speaking English, the whole thing is done by the contrast of vowels you might almost say.

Weir of Hermiston
ROBERT LOUIS STEVENSON

For a moment Hermiston warmed his hands at the fire, presenting his back to Archie; then suddenly disclosed on him the terrors
of the Hanging Face.

'What's this I hear of ye?' he asked.

There was no answer possible to Archie.

'. . . I hear that at the hanging of Duncan Jopp – and, man! ye
had a fine client there – in the middle of all the riffraff of the ceety,
ye thought fit to cry out, "This is a damned murder, and my gorge
rises at the man that haangit him."'

'No, sir, these were not my words,' cried Archie.

'What were yer words, then?' asked the judge.

'I believe I said, "I denounce it as a murder!"' said the son. 'I
beg your pardon – a God-defying murder. I have no wish to
conceal the truth,' he added, and looked his father for a moment
in the face.

'There was nothing about your gorge rising, then?'

'That was afterwards, my lord, as I was leaving the Speculative.
I said I had been to see the miserable creature hanged, and my
gorge rose at it.'

'You're a young gentleman that doesna approve of caapital
punishment,' said Hermiston. 'Weel, I'm an auld man that does. I
was glad to get Jopp haangit, and for what would I pretend I
wasna? You're all for honesty, it seems; you wouldn't even
steik your mouth on the public street. What for should I steik
mines upon the Bench, the King's officer, bearing the sword, a
dreid to evil-doers, as I was from the beginning, and as I will be
to the end! Mair than enough of it! Heedious! I never gave twa
thoughts heediousness, I have no call to be bonny. I'm a
man that gets through with my day's business, and let that
suffice.'

The ring of sarcasm had died out of his voice as he went on, the
plain words became invested with some of the dignity of the
Justice-seat. 'It would be telling you if you could say as much,' the
speaker resumed. 'But ye cannot. Ye've been reading some of my
cases, ye say. But it was not for the law in them, it was to spy out
your faither's nakedness, a fine employment in a son. You're

splairging; you're running at lairge in life like a wild nowt to the Bar. You're not fit for it; no splairger is . . .'

'. . . Father, let me go to the Peninsula,' said Archie. 'That's all I'm fit for – to fight . . .'

'. . . I think not,' continued Hermiston. 'And I would send no man to be a servant to the King, God bless him! that has proved such a shauchling son to his own faither. You can splairge here on Edinburgh street, and where's the hairm? It doesna play buff on me! And if there were twenty thousand eediots like yourself, sorrow a Duncan Jopp would hang the fewer. But there's no splairging in a camp; and if you were to go to it, you would find out for yourself whether Lord Well'n'ton approves of caapital punishment or not. You a sodger!' he cried, with a sudden burst of scorn. 'Ye auld wife, the sodgers would bray at ye like cuddies!' As at the drawing of a curtain, Archie was aware of some illogicality in his position, and stood abashed. He had a strong impression, besides, of the essential valour of the old gentleman before him, how conveyed it would be hard to say . . .

'. . . I have no other son, you see,' said Hermiston. A bonny one I have gotten! But I must just do the best I can wi' him, and what am I to do? If ye had been younger, I would have wheepit ye for this rideeculous exhibeetion. The way it is, I have just to grin and bear. But one thing is to be clearly understood. As a faither, I must grin and bear it; but if I had been the Lord Advocate instead of the Lord Justice-Clerk, son or no son, Mr Erchibald Weir would have been in a jyle the night.'

Readers: Iain Cuthbertson, Judy Cornwell

Full Selection:
Sun Rising, JOHN DONNE
Sonnet 116, WILLIAM SHAKESPEARE
A, B and C, STEPHEN LEACOCK
Mezeray's History of France, MATTHEW PRIOR
Musée des Beaux Arts, W. H. AUDEN
Boswell's Johnson
Pride and Prejudice, JANE AUSTEN
A slice of Wedding Cake, ROBERT GRAVES

Weir of Hermiston, ROBERT LOUIS STEVENSON
During Wind and Rain, THOMAS HARDY
The Sunlight on the Garden, LOUIS MACNEICE

FRANK DELANEY

1984

Frank Delaney is a clever man to have built such a good career out of what gives him such great pleasure, reading and talking about books. He helped create Radio 4's 'Bookshelf' programme, and presented it for its first five years, during which time he interviewed 1200 authors. It must have been a daunting workload, however enjoyable the reading may have been. Fortunately for him, he has one of those wonderful memories that can recall a phrase, read sometimes many years previously, exactly apposite to the subject in hand. His 'With Great Pleasure', recorded as part of the Lancaster Literary Festival, was the first I produced on taking over the series. It was very popular, both with the audience in the theatre and the audience at home. However I had the benefit of an extra show, the sight of Frank Delaney and the actor T. P. McKenna trying to outdo each other in miming the gaits of various characters commonly seen in the vicinity of Dublin pubs.

Anybody with an Irish accent choosing is expected, obliged, to include the ineluctable William Butler Yeats – not mind you the 'Lake Isle of Innisfree', what Dr Leavis called 'that unfortunate poem' because it was anthologised so much. I've chosen as a beginning and an end as it were one short poem which is economical, but rich and final in what it says. It's Yeats at his best, I believe, on his best subject – love.

The Pity of Love
W. B. YEATS

A pity beyond all telling
Is hid in the heart of love;
The folk who are buying and selling,
The clouds on their journey above,
The cold winds ever blowing,
And the shadowy hazel grove
Where mouse-grey waters are flowing,
Threaten the head that I love.

Given that Yeats never finally 'got it together' with Maud Gonne MacBride, his fellow Dublin men would say 'Ah sure, what would he know about it?' But there is a point in that poem; you see the point about the Irish is when we talk a lot we may actually say very little, but when we talk very little we may actually be saying a lot. This characteristic stems as much from language as from temperament. Yeats wrote entirely in English, to his regret, because the original Gaelic spoken in Ireland is at once marvellously obfuscating and lucid – ideal for poetry, and of course at the same time the exemplar of the living Celtic paradox. But unfortunately today that language, that Erse, has taken a pounding over the years and is now in danger of being beached by the tide of English language which sweeps over the island.

A young Irish poet called Aidan Carl Matthews packed the whole idea into a three line poem.

A Marginal Gloss on the Death of Irish
AIDAN CARL MATTHEWS

The tide gone out for good,
Thirty-one words for seaweed
Whiten on the foreshore.

Thirty-one words for seaweed! How many words I wonder for love? Growing up in Ireland I always knew when love was taking place if, on a Sunday afternoon, when a couple walked out together, he, silently, but eloquently, was wheeling her bicycle.

When I was a small boy around the fat acres of County Tipperary, I was a voyeur. Love in all its forms interested me, the hope of seeing lovers kissing or even meeting was electric – and I didn't even know that I should tell it in confession.

There is a phrase that comes to mind which recalls an early ambition of mine. The phrase is in the second verse of 'Fern Hill' by Dylan Thomas, that Welshman who, if he had learnt to swim, could have been an Irishman. The line was 'And as I was green and carefree, famous among the barns'. I wanted to be famous among the barns, not as a lover because I was still terrified of the parish priest. I wanted to be famous as, perhaps, a legendary huntsman, or a farmer known for being a shrewd judge of cattle, or a ploughman with a straight eye and a steady hand.

I grew up in the province of Munster in the 1940s and '50s. The new nation of the south was poor, but hopeful and it was desperate for self knowledge and respectability. I am no huntsman, can't plough, was too poor to farm. But there was one way to become famous among the barns in those days, and that was to acquire a reputation for learning. A century before me a romantic and gaunt figure stalked the land whom I thought I might one day emulate. The poet Pardraic Colum captured him.

A Poor Scholar of the Forties
PADRAIC COLUM

My eyelids red and heavy are
With bending o'er the smouldering peat.
I know the Aeneid now by heart,
My Virgil read in cold and heat,
In loneliness and hunger smart;
    And I know Homer, too, I ween,
    As Munster poets know Ossian.

And I must walk this road that winds
'Twixt bog and bog, while east there lies
A city with its men and books;
With treasures open to the wise,
Heart-words from equals, comrade-looks;
    Down here they have but tale and song.
    They talk Repeal the whole night long.

'You teach Greek verbs and Latin nouns,'
The dreamer of Young Ireland said,

'You do not hear the muffled call,
The sword being forged, the far-off tread
Of hosts to meet as Gael and Gall –
   What good to us your wisdom-store
   Your Latin verse, your Grecian Lore?'

And what to me is Gael or Gall?
Less than the Latin of the Greek –
I teach these by the dim rush-light
In smoky cabins night and week.
But what avail my teaching slight?
   Years hence, in rustic speech, a phrase,
   As in wild earth a Grecian Vase!

But that poem, learned with joy in school, also aroused great conflicts in me. Political words those: 'Repeal' meant repeal of the Act of Union, the 'sword being forged' meant war, Gael and Gall Irish versus foreigner. Deep within my bones lay the old feelings for this strange green island I lived on, with its sense of the happy-grotesque. Yet my intake in print was all in the English language and usually emanating from England, though it would be too much of an exaggeration to say that I was becoming culturally English while remaining emotionally Irish. Coming as I did from a male-dominated society, the most exciting revelation I had in the five years of presenting 'Bookshelf' on Radio 4, that doughty son of the Home Service, was the manner in which writing by women had become so important at this point in the century. The list of authors whose books struck chords is a long list – earlier, Rebecca West, Elizabeth Bowen, Virginia Woolf, then Rosamund Lehmann, Storm Jameson followed by Iris Murdoch, Margaret Drabble, Elizabeth Jane Howard, Susan Hill, Judith Burnley, Edna O'Brien.

Their statements collectively, for me at any rate, put the labels on our society in a way in which we can all read them. In assessing the mood which their books created in me, and in the context of this anthology, I was looking for one simple way in which to consider their obvious solitary commitment to what they do. And I found it in the works of one of their predecessors.

Autumn
CHRISTINA ROSSETTI

I dwell alone – I dwell alone, alone,
Whilst full my river flows down to the sea,
   Gilded with flashing boats
     That bring no friend to me:
O love-songs, gurgling from a hundred throats,
     O love-pangs, let me be.

Fair fall the freighted boats which gold and stone
     And spices bear to sea:
Slim, gleaming maidens swell their mellow notes,
     Love-promising, entreating –
      Ah! sweet, but fleeting –
    Beneath the shivering, snow-white sails.
Hush! the wind flags and fails –

Hush! they will lie becalmed in sight of strand –
   Sight of my strand, where I do dwell alone:
Their songs wake singing echoes in my land –
   They cannot hear me moan.

   One latest, solitary swallow flies
   Across the sea, rough autumn-tempest tost,
   Poor bird, shall it be lost?
Dropped down into this uncongenial sea,
     With no kind eyes
     To watch it while it dies,
    Unguessed, uncared for, free:
      Set free at last,
      The short pang past,
In sleep, in death, in dreamless sleep locked fast.

Mine avenue is all a growth of oaks,
     Some rent by thunder-strokes,
Some rustling leaves and acorns in the breeze;
     Fair fall my fertile trees,
That rear their goodly heads, and live at ease.

A spider's web blocks all mine avenue;
   He catches down and foolish painted flies,

That spider wary and wise.
Each morn it hangs a rainbow strung with dew
   Betwixt boughs green with sap.
    So fair, few creatures guess it is a trap:
     I will not mar the web.
Tho' sad I am to see the small lives ebb.

It shakes – my trees shake – for a wind is roused
    In cavern where it housed:
     Each white and quivering sail,
    Of boats among the water leaves
Hollows and strains in the full-throated gale;
     Each maiden sings again –
Each languid maiden sings again –
Had lulled to sleep with rest of spice and balm.
    Miles down my river to the sea
     They float and wane,
    Long miles away from me.
    Perhaps they say: 'She grieves,
     Uplifted, like a beacon, on her tower.'
    Perhaps they say: 'One hour
More, and we dance among the golden sheaves.'
    Perhaps they say: 'One hour
     More, and we stand,
     Face to face, hand in hand;
Make haste, O slack gale, to the looked-for land!'

    My trees are not in flower,
     I have no bower,
    And gusty creaks my tower,
And lonesome, very lonesome, is my strand.

Readers: Barbara Jefford, T. P. McKenna

Full Selection:
The Pity of Love, W. B. YEATS
A Marginal Gloss on the Death of Irish, AIDAN CARL MATTHEWS
Sonnet from The Portugese, ELIZABETH BARRETT BROWNING
Meeting at Night, ROBERT BROWNING
How to Grow a Wisteria, EDNA O'BRIEN

Windy Nights, ROBERT LOUIS STEVENSON
A Poor Scholar of the Forties, PADRAIC COLUM
Miss Knightsbridge, CANDIDA LYCETT-GREEN
Meeting Point, LOUIS MACNEICE
Autumn, CHRISTINA ROSETTI
The Power and the Glory, GRAHAM GREENE
Ulysses, JAMES JOYCE
If You Ever Go to Dublin, PATRICK KAVANAGH
After-Meeting, CHRISTY BROWN

LORD DENNING

1981

The generally wise, frequently controversial and always venerable figure of the Master of the Rolls possessed, on the evidence of this programme, a personality of great warmth and robust humour. His selection was wide-ranging, showing a strong preference for the classics of English literature: Wordsworth, Browning, Jane Austen, Dickens, Betjeman, Shakespeare, Masefield, Kipling and so on. If there were few surprises, no real quirkiness, that is not to say that in making his selection Lord Denning merely fell back on to a half-remembered introduction to literature from his schooldays. On the contrary, it is clear that throughout his programme the items and authors chosen were those that after a lifetime of reading he genuinely loved the best.

This evening I am going to throw all the law books out of the window. I have left them in my library the other side of the river. They are not fit to be read aloud – or at all. We are going to read to you some works of literature. In doing so I shall be following the advice of Sir Walter Scott in his novel *Guy Mannering*. When the lay clerk went into the lawyer's chambers, he found the walls lined, not with law books but with books of history and literature – the great authors – and on the walls a portrait or two. The lawyer, pointing to the books of history and literature, says: 'These are my tools of trade. A lawyer without history of litera- ture is a mechanic, a mere working mason; if he have some knowledge of these, he may venture to call himself an architect.'

So there – let's be architects, but first a little bit of prose of my own. I'm going to tell you of a letter which I received a little while ago from a student. He knew I was Master of the Rolls. This is what he wrote from International Students' House in London:

Dear Lord Denning,
I am an Indian citizen. I graduated in mechanical engineering in the University of London and was awarded a Master of Science degree. I feel I have the necessary qualifications, motivation, energy, drive and personality to begin a successful career in an automobile industry. I will ever remain grateful to you if you will kindly help me to begin my professional career with your company, the Rolls Royce Motor Company.

I notice we have the Vicar here. He might like another little story of mine. This is when a Lord Bishop went to the Temple Church in London, where the lawyers congregate and the acoustics are not at all good. The Verger said to the Bishop, 'Pray, my Lord, speak very clearly and distinctly because the agnostics here are terrible.'

I expect that all of you know from childhood – as I do – the charming piece by Leigh Hunt about Abou Ben Adhem. It was a favourite of my dear friend and great advocate, Norman Birkett. Lady Denning used to recite it too when she was young.

Abou Ben Adhem
LEIGH HUNT

Abou Ben Adhem (may his tribe increase!)
   Awoke one night from a deep dream of peace,
And saw, within the moonlight in his room,
Making it rich, and like a lily in bloom,

An angel writing in a book of gold:-
Exceeding peace had made Ben Adhem bold,
And to the presence in the room he said,
  'What writest thou?' – The vision rais'd its head,
And with a look made of all sweet accord,
Answer'd, 'The names of those who love the Lord.'
  'And is mine one?' said Abou. 'Nay, not so,'
Replied the angel. Abou spoke more low,
But cheerly still; and said, 'I pray thee, then,
Write me as one that loves his fellow men.'
  The angel wrote, and vanish'd. The next night
It came again with a great wakening light,
And show'd the names whom love of God had blest,
And lo! Ben Adhem's name led all the rest.

Some people have said that my style of writing is similar to that of Lord Macaulay. I don't think so myself, but if I have been influenced by it, it is quite unconscious. I have always admired his writing and particularly the passage in which he describes the trial of Warren Hastings, when he appeared before the House of Lords on a charge of corruption in India.

Warren Hastings' Trial
LORD MACAULAY

Hastings advanced to the bar, and bent his knee. The culprit was indeed not unworthy of that great presence. He had ruled an extensive and populous country, and made laws and treaties, had sent forth armies, had set up and pulled down princes. And in his high place he had so borne himself, that all had feared him, that most had loved him, and that hatred itself could deny him no title to glory, except virtue. He looked like a great man, and not like a bad man. A person small and emaciated, yet deriving dignity from a carriage which, while it indicated deference to the court, indicated also habitual self-possession and self-respect, a high intellectual forehead, a brow pensive, but not gloomy, a mouth of inflexible decision, a face pale and worn, but serene, on which was written, as legibly as under the picture in the council-chamber at Calcutta, *Mens aequa in arduis*; such was the aspect with which the great proconsul presented himself to his judges.

Each year – early in May – I go to a beautiful set of almshouses in Greenwich. They were founded 400 years ago by my predecessor, the Master of the Rolls at that time. I preach a sermon to the elderly ones there, some older than me. But I am no good at sermons. It being a lovely spring day I sometimes recite to them the words of Robert Browning which express our springtime better than any.

Home Thoughts from Abroad
ROBERT BROWNING

O to be in England
Now that April's there,
And whoever wakes in England
Sees, some morning, unaware,
That the lowest boughs and the brushwood sheaf
Round the elm-tree bole are in tiny leaf,
While the chaffinch sings on the orchard bough
In England – now!

And after April, when May follows,
And the whitethroat builds, and all the swallows!
Hark, where my blossom'd pear-tree in the hedge
Leans to the field and scatters on the clover
Blossoms and dewdrops – at the bent spray's edge –
That's the wise thrush; he sings each song twice over,
Lest you should think he never could recapture
That first fine careless rapture!
And though the fields look rough with hoary dew,
All will be gay when noontide wakes anew
The buttercups, the little children's dower
– Far brighter than this gaudy melon-flower.

I always enjoy Charles Dickens, especially *Pickwick Papers*, and the trial of Bardell against Pickwick. But I prefer the time when Mr Pickwick and Sam Weller took the London coach to Ipswich. They stayed at the Great White Horse. When they went to bed, Mr Pickwick got into a room with double beds which he thought was his own. He put on his night-cap and was about to get undressed when a person with a candle came in and sat down at a dressing-table. It was a four-poster bed – he slipped behind the curtains with his head just peeping out and looked out to see who was there.

Pickwick Papers
CHARLES DICKENS

Mr Pickwick almost fainted with horror and dismay. Standing before the dressing-glass was a middle-aged lady, in yellow curl-papers, busily engaged in brushing what ladies call their 'back-hair'. However the unconscious middle-aged lady came into that room, it was quite clear that she contemplated remaining there for the night; for she had brought a rushlight and shade with her, which, with praiseworthy caution against fire, she had stationed in a basin on the floor, where it was glimmering away, like a gigantic lighthouse in a particularly small piece of water. 'Bless my soul,' thought Mr Pickwick, 'what a dreadful thing!'

'Hem!' said the lady; and in went Mr Pickwick's head with automaton-like rapidity.

'I never met with anything so awful as this,' thought poor Mr Pickwick, the cold perspiration starting in drops upon his night-cap. 'Never. This is fearful . . .'

'This matter is growing alarming,' reasoned Mr Pickwick with himself.

'I can't allow things to go on in this way. By the self-possession of the lady it is clear to me that I must have come into the wrong room. If I call out she'll alarm the house; but if I remain here the consequences will be still more frightful.'. . .

He shrank behind the curtains, and called out very loudly:

'Ha – hum!' . . .

'Gracious Heaven!' said the middle-aged lady, 'what's that?'

'It's – its – only a gentleman, Ma'am, said Mr Pickwick from behind the curtains.

'A gentleman!' said the lady with a terrific scream.

'It's all over!' thought Mr Pickwick.

'A strange man!' shrieked the lady . . .

'Ma'am,' said Mr Pickwick, thrusting out his head, in the extremity of his desperation, 'Ma'am . . .'

'Wretch,' said the lady, covering her eyes with her hands, 'what do you want here?'

'Nothing, Ma'am; nothing whatever, Ma'am;' said Mr Pickwick earnestly.

Mr Pickwick then tried to explain that he must have mistaken this bedroom for his own.

'If this improbable story be really true, sir,' said the lady, sobbing violently, 'you will leave it instantly.'

'I will, Ma'am, with the greatest pleasure,' replied Mr Pickwick.

'Instantly, sir,' said the lady.

'Certainly, Ma'am,' interposed Mr Pickwick very quickly. 'Certainly, Ma'am. I – I am very sorry, Ma'am,' said Mr Pickwick, making his appearance at the bottom of the bed, 'to have been the innocent occasion of this alarm and emotion; deeply sorry, Ma'am.'

The lady pointed to the door. One excellent quality of Mr Pickwick's character was beautifully displayed at this moment, under the most trying circumstances. Although he had hastily put on his hat over his night-cap, after the manner of the old patrol; although he carried his shoes and gaiters in his hand, and his coat and waistcoat over his arm; nothing could subdue his native politeness.

'I am exceedingly sorry, Ma'am,' said Mr Pickwick, bowing very low.

'If you are, sir, you will at once leave the room,' said the lady.

'Immediately, Ma'am; this instant, Ma'am,' said Mr Pickwick, opening the door, and dropping both his shoes with a crash in so doing.

'I trust, Ma'am,' resumed Mr Pickwick, gathering up his shoes, and turning round to bow again: 'I trust, Ma'am, that my unblemished character, and the devoted respect I entertain for your sex, will plead as some slight excuse for this.' – but before Mr Pickwick could conclude the sentence the lady had thrust him into the passage, and locked and bolted the door behind him.

Readers: Jill Balcon, Paul Rogers

Full Selection:
Abou Ben Adhem, LEIGH HUNT

GERALD DURRELL

1976

Many years ago, reading for the first time 'My Family and Other Animals' had me rattling the chair with laughter. At the time I had not heard of Gerald Durrell, not known that he was a very funny man who took great pleasure in the idiosyncrasies not only of his fellow men, but of all creatures, so the laughter contained an element of delighted surprise. The humour he conveys is not a trivialising one that sees wild creatures as somehow cute, but an essential element in his sharing with the reader his excitement at what he sees around him: 'I, in the days of my youth, used to read avidly every travel book that came my way, and I'd read something *called, you know, "Ninety Years in Tibet, with Sidelights on the Plant Life, Animal Life, Zoo Geography, Geology, Natives and their customs", and I'd read five hundred pages of this and I'd discover that this man had spent ninety years in Tibet and nothing funny had ever happened to him. So I swore to myself, having been bored by hundreds of these tomes, that if I ever wrote about travel I would try and write a little bit humorously.'*

I was brought up in Greece and I was mad on animals from the word go. My mother, who was a reasonably honest woman, once said to me that the first word I ever spoke was in fact 'zoo'. I have being saying it in terms of despair ever since.

When I lived in Greece I could keep pets and have fun. In that respect, the natural world was to me an open book, but I also had to read in order to explore it thoroughly and one of the very first people I read was the great French naturalist Jean Henri Fabre – an enormously important man in terms of my development, and indeed in terms of the development of natural history, because he was one of the first people who proved that you could examine the workings of creatures and interpret them in a poetical fashion in beautiful prose, which really meant something, so that you didn't have to be a scientist to appreciate what he was talking about.

The Life of the Caterpillar
J. H. FABRE

Physical science is today preparing to give us wireless telegraphy, by means of Hertzian waves. Can the Great Peacock have anticipated our efforts in this direction? In order to set the surrounding air in motion and to inform pretenders miles away, can the newly hatched bride have at her disposal electric or magnetic waves, which one sort of screen would arrest and another let through? In a word, does she, in her own manner, employ a kind of wireless telegraphy? I see nothing impossible in this: insects are accustomed to invent things quite as wonderful.

I therefore lodge the female in boxes of various characters. Some are made of tin, some of cardboard, some of wood. All are hermetically closed, are even sealed with stout putty. I also use a glass bell-jar standing on the insulating support of a pane of glass.

Well, under these conditions of strict closing, never a male arrives, not one, however favourable the mildness and quiet of the evening. No matter its nature, whether of metal or glass, of wood or cardboard, the closed receptacle forms an insuperable obstacle to the effluvia that betrays the captive's whereabouts. A layer of cotton two fingers thick gives the same result. I place the female in a large jar, tying a shoot of wadding over the mouth by way of a lid. This is enough to keep the neighbourhood in ignorance of the secrets of my laboratory. No male puts in an appearance.

On the other hand, make use of ill-closed cracked boxes, or even hide them in a drawer, in a cupboard; and, notwithstanding this added mystery, the Moths will arrive in numbers as great as when they come thronging to the trellised cage standing in full view on a table. I have retained a vivid recollection of an evening when the recluse was waiting in a hat-box at the bottom of a closed wall-cupboard. The Moths arrived, went to the door, struck it with their wings, knocked at it to express their wish to enter. Passing wayfarers, coming no one knows whence across the fields, they well knew what was inside there, behind those boards.

We must therefore reject the idea of any means of information similar to that of wireless telegraphy, for the first screen set up, whether a good conductor or a bad, stops the female's signals completely. To give these a free passage and carry them to a distance, one condition is indispensable: the receptacle in which the female is contained must be imperfectly closed, so as to establish a communication between the inner and the outer air. This brings us back to the probability of an odour, though that was contradicted by my experiment with naphthaline.

Fabre had an enormous effect on me as a young naturalist at the age of seven to ten. I read him avidly and he led me, as it were, by the hand into the undergrowth to observe insects and to learn how to observe them in fact.

I lived a fairly unconventional life in Greece, one way and another. I was allowed to do and read pretty well anything that I liked, and I lived a very interesting life in the sense that I lived in two worlds; by virtue of the currency in those days we were what could be described as multi-millionaires, and the sort of society that we moved in were multi-millionaires, but at the same time all my friends were among the peasants, so I saw real poverty on the one hand, and riches on the other hand. And I also had a very eccentric family who had eccentric friends, and this again opened up new windows to me. I also had a series of very extraordinary tutors, because I didn't have any conventional training as far as education was concerned. Even now I have difficulty signing my name with a cross. But I had these remarkable tutors who discovered that the only way they could teach me, in fact, was to teach me through animals. Everything had to be geared to animals; if they wanted to teach me mathematics for example they had to work out things like: 'If it takes a caterpillar six weeks to eat one leaf, how long will it take forty-six caterpillars to . . .' You know, all that sort of stuff. And my family's approach to life was very astringent and, I think, unconventionally good from the point of view of somebody who's growing up. I remember my mother once saying, in terms of despair almost, 'Why is it that we always think other people are peculiar?' and my brother replying 'Because they are.'

I think that poets by and large are failed naturalists. They seem to see our kinship with nature much more clearly than the average novelist. You can read page after page of interminable kitchen-sink stuff, where so-and-so's sleeping with so-and-so or going out with so-and-so, or so-and-so's reacting with so-and-so, and they never have a sentence which tells you that there's a sparrow chirping on the roof; which rather gives you the feeling that everything is kitchen sink. Whereas the poets do take you out of that, and have a much sharper eye in putting us into our context. We tend to step out of our context now. We've stepped out of nature and we're pretending to be God, which is a rather dangerous thing to do, and the poets, I think, push us back into where we belong. Now John Donne, who's probably one of the most moving, the most virile of the English poets, uses with incredible effect in a love poem, of all things a small parasite as a symbol of love.

The Flea
JOHN DONNE

Mark but this flea, and mark in this,
How little that which thou deny'st me is;
It suck'd me first, and now sucks thee,
And in this flea, our two bloods mingled be;
Thou know'st that this cannot be said
A sin, nor shame, nor loss of maidenhead,
    Yet this enjoys before it woo,
      And pamper'd swells with one blood made of two,
      And this, alas, is more than we would do.

Oh stay, three lives in one flea spare,
Where we almost, yea more than married are.
This flea is you and I, and this
Our marriage bed, and marriage temple is;
Though parents grudge, and you, we're met,
And cloister'd in these living walls of jet.
    Though use make you apt to kill me,
      Let not to that, self-murder added be,
      And sacrilege, three sins in killing three.

Cruel and sudden, hast thou since
Purpled thy nail, in blood of innocence?
Wherein could this flea guilty be,
Except in that drop which it suck'd from thee?
Yet thou triumph'st, and say's that thou
Finds't not thyself, nor me, the weaker now;
    'Tis true, then learn how false, fears be;
      Just so much honor, when thou yield'st to me,
      Will waste, as this flea's death took life from thee.

My brother suffered much at my hands when I was young. As far as animal life was concerned, he always seemed to be bearing the brunt of whatever pets I happened to have. He was always being pecked by magpies or having an owl descend on his head when he least expected it, or a scorpion fall out of a matchbox, that sort of thing. So he really was not a great lover of animal life. But even he, as a poet, can be good.

I must admit this, albeit reluctantly, and this very short poem by him contains, I think, some very lovely images.

The Cicada
LAWRENCE DURRELL

Transparent sheath of the dead cicada,
The eyes stay open like a dead Jap,
Financially no spongy parts to putrefy
Simply snap off the scaly integument of mica.
You could make a tiny violin of such a body,
Lanterns for elves, varnish into brooches
And wear by lamplight this transparent stare of noon,
In gold or some such precious allegorical metal,
Which spells out the dead wine which follows soon.

Even my brother has moments.

Actually I shouldn't be rude about him because he has always helped and encouraged me. In fact it was he that really wanted me to be a writer, and not get mixed up with animals. He was always encouraging me to write even when I was young, and he's always been very proud of any progress that I've made. People always think that because there are two writers in the family there must be some sort of rivalry between them, but in this particular instance there isn't. I just simply tell him that he writes great literature and I write books that people read . . .

Readers: Geoffrey Collins, Anne Rosenfeld

Full Selection:
The Life of the Caterpillar, J. H. FABRE
A Naturalist's Voyage Around the World CHARLES DARWIN
Mariana, ALFRED, LORD TENNYSON
The Flea, JOHN DONNE
The Cicada, LAWRENCE DURRELL
Travels in West Africa, MARY KINGSLEY
Winnie the Pooh, A. A. MILNE
An Attractive Impediment, PATRICK CAMPBELL
The Journey's Echo, FREYA STARK

SEAN O'FAOLAIN

1970

When a poet or other writer presents 'With Great Pleasure', he or she generally makes an honest attempt to be self-revealing and entertaining. It seldom, however, contains writing of the quality that made him or her famous in the first place. It would be unfair to expect it to do so. The style of the programme is deliberately informal, a conversation with the audience. Indeed the presenters frequently extemporise from notes rather than deliver a fully fledged script. Sean O' Faolain, however, managed to maintain informality whilst from the first sentence leaving us in no doubt we were in the presence of a mind of poetic drive and sinew.

Of all the countless words that we may remember from our early reading I think the least interesting are those we remember most easily – words that lie on the surface of our minds, that can pop up as effortlesly as a piece of toast out of a toaster – apt quotations for any chance occasion. The words I would like to resurrect here are deeper rooted, pieces of prose or verse that were planted in me by experience that it takes a conscious effort to recall, words that have become so much part of my purely instinctive being that they're like past pastures and cuds chewed long ago by some old ruminant animal who lives in a perpetual Now.

I was born in Cork in 1900 which makes me a man of the twenties. Meaning the 1820s – like Yeats, our last romantic: Shelley, Keats, Byron and all that, on to the pre-Raphaelites, Blake, Matthew Arnold. In other words, I grew up simple, sensuous and passionate in a nineteenth-century country town, differing only in so far as Dublin was and still is a somewhat larger nineteenth-century country town. In Cork the green hills walked down into the streets and the Atlantic flowed into them, sometimes literally, yet leaving us all in our smoky little valley with just enough of the oppressiveness of city life to make us relish the beauty, the escape, the release of the surrounding countryside. So, even if Cork was not Oxford, or Paris or London, feverishly intellectual or breathlessly competitive, it was inevitable that I should fall in love with English pastoral poetry, as a very young man with The Scholar Gypsy's abjurations to fly from the feverish contact of the busy world whose 'mental strife, though it gives no bliss yet spoils our rest'.

The Scholar Gypsy
MATTHEW ARNOLD

Then fly our greetings, fly our speech and smiles!
    – As some grave Tyrian trader, from the sea,
      Described at sunrise an emerging prow
Lifting the cool-hair'd creepers stealthily,
      The fringes of a southward-facing brow
        Among the Aegean isles;
And saw the merry Grecian coaster come,
      Freighted with amber grapes, and Chian wine,
      Green bursting figs, and tunnies steep'd in brine;
And knew the intruders on his ancient home.

The young light-hearted Masters of the waves;
      And snatched his rudder, and shook out more sail,
      And day and night held on indignantly
O'er the blue Midland waters with the gale,
      Betwixt the Syrtes and soft Sicily,
        To where the Atlantic raves
Outside the Western Straits, and unbent sails
      There, where down cloudy cliffs, through sheets of foam,
      Shy traffickers, the dark Iberians come;
And on the beach undid his corded bales.

Like so much of nineteenth-century nature poetry – and how odd that phrase 'nature poetry' sounds today! – 'The Scholar Gypsy' had one great drawback for me. It evoked the scenery, the details of life, even the ethos of another civilisation. If Cork was not Arnold's Oxford, alas!, neither, alas, was his Oxfordshire my County Cork. The furniture of the poem kept it as remote from me as Russia. Inglenooked alehouses, mossy barns, maidens dancing around ancient elms in May, nightingales, dingles – I had to look up that word in a dictionary – 'the line of festal lights in Christ Church Hall'. If it is true that the most difficult thing for any youth to do is to see life with his own eyes, it's also true that he carries on the bridge of his nose clotted eye-filters bequeathed to him by his elders. Poetry like Arnold's, for me, at that time, was enchanting but it was also emollient, escapist and ultimately unrevealing.

My Book of Revelation – I still have it, the spine gone, the pages dog-eared and foxed – was Kuno Meyer's translations from the Old Irish. Here I found poetry that was recognisable in every detail, at its best particular, almost always dramatic and personal. The words 'I' and 'me' are all over Irish poetry. It is our ethnic tendency, perhaps, to dramatise; and it makes for objectivity; and it saves us from what T. S. Eliot thought one of the weaknesses of all nineteenth-century English poetry – its habit of ruminating self-indulgently.

Here are a few verses from the long poem 'King and Hermit' where simply in order that the poet may present his nature poem as a little one-act play, the king is made to ask the hermit why he is a hermit. And the hermit's answer is the poem.

King and Hermit
Old Irish trans. KUNO MEYER

I have chosen a hut in the wood
Because nobody sees it but God,
Between a hazel and an ash,
With a tall pine over it.

The kindly coloured summer
Pours into my dish
Pignuts, leeks and marjoram,
Morning sweet and fresh.

My music is the humming
Of tiny bees and chafers,
Or the woodcock and the geese
Drumming through the rain,

When the winter wails
Through the woven wood,
And the clouded waterfalls
Dull the whooping swans.

Here, free from strife and fighting
I can praise the King, my God,
Who fills my wood
With everything that's good.

A simple, spare, concrete, intimate, ungeneralised close-up. With scores of such poems in my mind I could, under the carved arch of any ruined Romanesque churchlet, deep in docks, nettles, mallow, cowdung, neglect and tinkers' rags, blend myself into ancestral memories of my own people.

It was the same with love poems. For every youth every love poem was written specially for him and her alone. He turns every love poem into a mirror of his desire. I may have, in self-protection, laughed with my friends over Meredith's 'Love in a Valley'. In secret I adored it.

Love in the Valley
GEORGE MEREDITH

Shy as the squirrel and wayward as the swallow,
    Swift as the swallow along the river's light
Circleting the surface to meet his mirrored winglets
    Fleeter she seems in her stay than in her flight.
Shy as the squirrel that leaps among the pinetops,
    Wayward as the swallow overhead at set of sun,
She whom I love is hard to catch and conquer,
    Hard, but O the glory of the winning were she won!

Two dozen idyllic, dancing verses of it, mightily affective for the springtime of youth, but though its sentiments are unassailable, all passionate feeling is held off – like the swallow in that excellent image, 'circleting the surface to meet his mirrored winglets . . . along the river's light'. So that very soon, when hot desire fanned love to passion and, as all young men do at that stage, I was wondering what on earth to do about it all, I began to think it a carminative poem – that lovely adjective (in case you do not happen to know) simply means any medicine that lets the gas out of you.

Besides, Meredith, like Arnold, expected more stock responses than I, as an alien, could give to the inevitable red-roofed 'mossed old farmhouse', the cottage garden with its dainty tulips and lilies (tulips I might manage but lilies were beyond my means), the boys playing cricket on the village green, the white owl curving through the dusk, the doves among the fir trees that 'through the long noon coo, crooning through the coo'. These furnishings were all elements in an enviable tradition of civil living in an island that had not been invaded since William the Conqueror. They were, in Henry James's words about Nathaniel Hawthorne – a writer whose unfinished environment I was better fitted to understand – all part of 'the dense, richer, warmer European spectacle' that I would not share for many years to come.

'Love in the Valley' is a charming love poem but it is far removed from the wilder passions proper to our natural environment, our tradition, as the half-tamed barbarians that, at our best and worst, we so splendidly are.

After Nature and love my generation found its greatest release through political revolt. Politics and poetry, however, have never been fertile bedfellows, until, after the event, when the poet goes to bed with a memory or a ghost. I know that I read all Shelley's rebellious poetry during those troubled years. I remember being held up by a British patrol in Cork, on a bridge at midnight, and how the young lieutenant in charge drew from my pocket a small blue volume – which I still have. He flashed his torch on the title, *The Poems of Shelley*, returned it and with a faint smile said, 'Pass on!' I almost thought he was going to add, 'Friend'. I see that in this little volume I wrote the words *fine stuff* beside 'The Mask of Anarchy' and the 'Ode to Liberty'. They are certainly not part of my flower-garden today. If those poems are not in Wyndham Lewis's anthology of bad poetry, *The Stuffed Owl*, they should be.

I Met Murder on the Way

P. B. SHELLEY

I met murder on the way –
He had a mask like Castlereagh –
Very smooth he looked and grim;
Seven bloodhounds followed him.

All were fat and well they might
Be in admirable plight,
For one by one and two by two
He tossed them human hearts to chew . . .

And the little children who
Around his feet played to and fro
Thinking every tear a gem
Had their brains knocked out of them . . .

Yeats was more suitable for us than Shelley but Yeats, unfortunately, did not publish his finest patriotic poems, such as 'Easter 1916' or 'Sixteen Dead Men', until 1921, but he did publish one blazing poem that we all knew in 1914 – following the death of his old Fenian friend John O'Leary and Jim Larkin's gallant but doomed Tramway Strike in 1913.

September 1913

W. B. YEATS

What need you, being come to sense,
But fumble in a greasy till
And add the halfpence to the pence
And prayer to shivering prayer, until
You have dried the marrow from the bone?
For men were born to pray and save:
Romantic Ireland's dead and gone,
It's with O'Leary in the grave.

Yet they were of a different kind
The names that stilled your childish play,
They have gone about the world like wind,
But little time had they to pray
For whom the hangman's rope was spun.

And what, God help us, could they save?
Romantic Ireland's dead and gone,
It's with O'Leary in the grave.

Was it for this the wild geese spread
The grey wing upon every tide;
For this that all the blood was shed,
For this Edward Fitzgerald died,
And Robert Emmet and Wolfe Tone,
All that delirium of the brave?
Romantic Ireland's dead and gone,
It's with O'Leary in the grave.

Yet could we turn the years again,
And call those exiles as they were
In all their loneliness and pain,
You'd cry, 'Some woman's yellow hair
Has maddened every mother's son':
They weighed so lightly what they gave.
But let them be, they're dead and gone,
They're with O'Leary in the grave.

It may seem a strange wish to dine at journey's end with Pater and with Donne, and Daedalus. But in 'death's dream kingdom' as Eliot calls this world of ours, there are also many mansions and, like Keats, we must traverse them all, opening door after door, embracing all experience. It may be that what blends all these men together is the eternal note of sadness. And that was Arnold's phrase for Sophocles, who heard it long ago on the Aegaean, as Daedalus must have when he saw Icarus tumbling into the sea under the heat of the sun.

Reader: Ray McAnally

Full Selection:
The Scholar Gypsy, MATTHEW ARNOLD
King and Hermit Old Irish trans. KUNO MEYER
Love in the Valley, GEORGE MEREDITH

I Cannot Tear Myself in Two, TOMAS O'HUIGIN trans. FRANK O'CONNOR
I Met Murder on the Way, PERCY BYSSHE SHELLEY
September 1913, W. B. YEATS
Easter 1916, W. B. YEATS
Marius the Epicurean, PATER
The Progresse of the Soul, JOHN DONNE
Portrait of the Artist as a Young Man, JAMES JOYCE

CHRISTOPHER FRY

1986

As a schoolboy in the fifties and as an amateur actor in the sixties I grew up with Christopher Fry's verse plays and elegant translations of French playwrights. Both are still being performed constantly, both by amateurs and professional companies. Listening to a voice from the radio and imagining what that person behind it looks like frequently leads to astonishment on finding out that the speaker looks nothing like the figure imagined. So it was with Christopher Fry. Hearing his voice on the telephone and imagining someone rather tall and patrician, I was both surprised and delighted to find that he was shorter than I expected, with a genial appearance and manner, and looking at least fifteen years younger than his true age. His performance and hold of an audience were exemplary, for example taking care to laugh at jokes in the pieces – even though he knew them well and indeed had heard them a number of times in rehearsal – to encourage the audience to share in them more fully and hence laugh louder. It made for more pleasure for them and a better show for us. Although his place in the history of drama is assured, it seems he may have a further pleasure to offer. At the time of writing there is talk of a new play for radio.

Faced with putting together half-an-hour's worth of prose and verse brought out all the indecision in me. After seventy years of reading, seventy hours wouldn't have seemed too much; so, to narrow the range of choice, I began by leaving out almost all of the big guns – no Shakespeare or Tolstoy or Keats and so forth – and many other pleasurable ones, Charles Lamb for instance (when did you last read him?) or Sir Thomas Browne or, eccentrically perhaps, Carlyle. But it's prodigal to spend time telling you what I haven't chosen. The choice in the end was governed by a vague sense of chronology, and partly by some slight linking ideas – journeying is one, and visiting another.

It's easy enough to know where to begin: we can start with my starting to learn to read, the first steps of a long journey to follow. The first lessons, of course, must have been of the Cat on the Mat kind; I don't remember anything about that. But then my Aunt Ada put before me her copy of *Pilgrim's Progress*, given to her by her father for Christmas 1865. First of all I feasted on the illustrations – one hundred and two of them, and marvellous they were – and then the serious matter of reading began.

Here, from the second part of the book, is the description of how Christiana and the children came to the Enchanted Ground. There is a note at the bottom of the page explaining that 'the mist and darkness of this stage are consistent with the spirit of the enchanted scene. Worldly pleasure waves her magic wand, and bids a cloud of misty incense to arise, and mysterious darkness to descend; and under these influences the soul is induced to sleep the deadly sleep of oblivion and forgetfulness.'

This is how John Bunyan describes it.

Pilgrim's Progress
JOHN BUNYAN

By this time they were got to the Enchanted Ground, where the air naturally tended to make one drowsy: and that place was all grown over with briars and thorns, excepting here and there, where was an enchanted arbour, upon which if a man sits, or in which if a man sleeps, it is a question, say some, whether he shall ever rise or wake again in this world. Over this forest therefore they went, both one and another: Mr Great-heart went before, for that he was their guide, Mr Valiant-for-truth came behind, being rear-guard; for fear lest peradventure some fiend, or dragon, or giant, or thief, should fall upon their rear, and so do mischief. They went on here, each man with his sword drawn in his hand, for they knew it was a dangerous place. Also they cheered up one another, as well they could. Feeble-mind, Mr Great-heart commanded, should come up after him, and Mr Despondency was under the eye of Mr Valiant.

Now they had not gone far, but a great mist and darkness fell upon them all, so that they could scarce, for a great while, one see the other: wherefore they were forced for some time to feel for one another by words, for they walked not by sight. But any one must think that here was but sorry going for the best of them all; but how much worse was it for the women and children, who both of feet and heart were but tender. Yet so it was, that, through the encouraging words of him that led in the front, and of him that brought them up behind, they made a pretty good shift to wag along.

'They were forced for some time to feel for one another by words.' I suppose that is what writing is, what all human communication is. I think it's a malady of most writers to have the feeling from time to time that their publishers could be making a greater effort to push the sale of their books. So it's unexpected to find that when Sylvia Townsend Warner's publisher wrote lamenting that he hadn't sold more copies of some book of hers, she wrote that he should look at things differently.

From a Letter to Her Publisher
SYLVIA TOWNSEND WARNER

I don't think four thousand copies such a wretched sale. You should try to take a longer view of it. If you had sold four thousand female kittens, for instance, you would think you had done marvels.

Now that we're on to the subject of what the poet Gray called 'the tabby kind', I wish we had time for William Cowper's 'Retired Cat' who:

Recumbent at her ease, ere long,

And lulled by her own humdrum song,
She left the cares of life behind . . .

But first in the Catalogue of poets is T. S. Eliot. I met him for the
first time at almost exactly the time of the publication of *The Book of
Practical Cats*. I know it was then because the 1939 war had just
begun. I told him that I had thought of trying to join a Fire Brigade
in London, but had a poor head for heights. 'You should
specialise', he said, 'in basements.'

The Naming of Cats
T. S. ELIOT

The Naming of Cats is a difficult matter,
It isn't just one of your holiday games;
You may think at first I'm as mad as a hatter
When I tell you, a cat must have THREE DIFFERENT NAMES.
First of all, there's the name that the family use daily,
Such as Peter, Augustus, Alonzo or James,
Such as Victor or Jonathan, George or Bill Bailey –
All of them sensible everyday names.
There are fancier names if you think they sound sweeter,
Some are for gentlemen, some for the dames:
Such as Plato, Admetus, Electra, Demeter –
But all of them sensible everyday names.
But I tell you, a cat needs a name that's particular,
A name that's peculiar, and more dignified,
Else how can he keep up his tail perpendicular,
Or spread out his whiskers, or cherish his pride?
Of names of this kind I can give you a quorum,
Such as Munkustrap, Quaxo, or Coricopat,
Such as Bombalurina, or else Jellyorum –
Names that never belong to more than one cat.
But above and beyond there's still one name left over,
And that is the name that you never will guess;
The name that no human research can discover –
But THE CAT HIMSELF KNOWS, and will never confess.
When you notice a cat in profound meditation,
A reason, I tell you, is always the same;
His mind is engaged in a rapt contemplation

Of a thought, of the thought, of the thought of his name;
His ineffable effable
Effanineffable
Deep and inscrutable singular Name.

W. H. Hudson was both a journeyer and a visitor. In 1900 he visited Chichester, near my present home, and took the darkest view of the city. He found it 'profoundly depressing'. 'The depression,' he says, 'is probably the malady commonly known as "the Chichesters" from which many persons who visit this town are said to suffer.' I hope and believe he would have a very different opinion now.

There's so much of his writing about England that would be a pleasure to include here – from *Hampshire Days*, or *A Shepherd's Life* or *Nature in Downland*; but I've chosen a piece from his first book, a novel, *The Purple Land*, in which the hero, leaving his wife behind in Montevideo, sets out on horse-back to ride to a place two hundred miles away. He comes to a long, low house thatched with rushes, and asks to lodge there for the night.

The Purple Land
W. H. HUDSON

I was kindly received by a numerous family, consisting of the owner, his hoary-headed old mother-in-law, his wife, three sons, and five daughters, all grown up . . . Besides the people, there were dogs, cats, turkeys, ducks. geese, and fowls without number. Not content with all these domestic birds and beasts, they also kept a horrid, shrieking paraoquet, which the old woman was incessantly talking to, explaining to the others all the time, in little asides, what the bird said or wished to say, or rather, what she imagined it wished to say. There were also several tame young ostriches, always hanging about the big kitchen or living-room on the look-out for a brass thimble, or iron spoon, or other little metallic *bonne bouche* to be gobbled up when no one was looking. A pet armadillo kept trotting in and out, in and out, the whole evening, and a lame gull perpetually wailing for something to eat – the most persistent beggar I ever met in my life.

The people were very jovial and rather industrious for so indolent a country. The land was their own, the men tended the cattle

. . . while the women made cheeses, rising before daylight to milk the cows . . . There were also several small children, belonging, I believe, to the daughters, notwithstanding the fact that they were unmarried. I was greatly amazed at hearing the name of one of these youngsters. Such Christian names as Trinity, Heart of Jesus, Nativity, John of God, Conception, Ascension, Incarnation, are common enough, but these had scarcely prepared me to meet with a fellow-creature named – well, Circumcision!

The most astounding journeys of the human being were those voyages into the unknown – the discovery, for example, of 'North and South Americay', as Arthur Hugh Clough rhymes them in an untitled poem. Clough, who had so much brilliance when he was at school at Rugby under Dr Arnold, died at the age of 42, before his gifts had borne all the fruit they promised. I have sometimes thought that in his 'Amours de Voyage' he may have given that hint of a verse-line which Eliot followed up in 'The Cocktail Party' and 'The Elder Statesman'.

In this piece he speaks for all of us in asking 'How in heaven's name did Columbus get over?'

How in Heaven's Name Did Columbus Get Over?
ARTHUR HUGH CLOUGH

> How in heaven's name did Columbus get over,
> Is a pure wonder to me, I protest,
> Cabot and Raleigh too, that well-read rover,
> Frobisher, Dampier, Drake and the rest;
> Bad enough all the same,
> For them that after came;
> But in great heaven's name,
> How he should ever think
> That on the other brink
> Of this wild waste, terra firma should be,
> Is a pure wonder, I must say, to me.
>
> How a man should ever hope to get thither,
> Even if he knew there was another side,
> But to suppose he should come any hither,
> Sailing straight on into chaos untried:
> In spite of the motion,

Across the whole ocean,
To stick to the notion
That in some nook or bend
Of a sea without end,
He should find North and South America,
Was pure madness, indeed, I must say.

What if wise men had, as far back as Ptolemy,
Judged that the earth like an orange was round,
None of them ever said, Come along, follow me,
Sail to the West, and the East will be found.
Many a day before
Ever they'd come ashore
Of the San Salvador
Sadder and wiser men,
They'd have turned back again;
And that *he* did not, but did cross the sea,
Is a pure wonder, I must say, to me.

Tennyson's 'Ode to the Death of the Duke of Wellington' written while he was Poet Laureate moved me as a small boy. Over a century later there was another memorable laureate poem, John Betjeman's 'A Ballad of the Investiture 1969': and in it you will find the visiting, the journeying, the detail of historic event, and Betjeman's true voice, not a ceremoniously assumed one. The 'Harry' mentioned at the end of the first stanza is The Reverend H. A. Williams; at the time of the poem he was Fellow and Dean of the Chapel of Trinity College, Cambridge.

A Ballad of Investiture 1969
JOHN BETJEMAN

The moon was in the Cambridge sky
And bathed Great Court in silver light
When Hastings-Bass and Woods and I
And quiet Elizabeth, tall and white,
With that sure clarity of mind
Which comes to those who've truly dined,
Reluctant rose to say good-night;
And all of us were bathed the while
In the large moon of Harry's smile.

Then, sir, you said what shook me through
So that my courage almost fails:
'I want a poem out of you
On my Investiture in Wales.'
Leaving, you slightly raised your hand –
'And that,' you said, 'is a command.'
For years I wondered what to do
And now, at last, I've thought it better
To write a kind of rhyming letter.

Spring frocks, silk hats, at morning's prime,
One of a varied congregation
I glided out at breakfast time,
With Euston's Earl from Euston Station,
Through Willesden's bleak industrial parts,
Through Watford on to leafy Herts
Bound for a single destination.
Warwicks and Staffs were soaked in rain;
So was the open Cheshire plain.

The railway crossed the river Dee
Where Mary called the cattle home,
The wide marsh widened into sea,
The wide sea whitened into foam.
The green Welsh hills came steeply down
To many a cara-circled town –
Prestatyn, Rhyl – till here were we,
As mountains rose on either hand,
Awed strangers in a foreign land.

I can't forget the climbing street
Below Caernarvon's castle wall,
The dragon flag, the tramp of feet,
The gulls' perturbed, insistent call,
Bow-windowed house-fronts painted new,
Heads craning out to get a view,
A mounting tension stilling all –
And, once within the castle gate,
The murmuring hush of those who wait.

Wet banners flap: The sea mist clears.
Colours are backed by silver stone.
Moustached hereditary peers
Are ranged in rows behind the throne.
With lifted sword the rites begin.
Earl Marshal leads the victims in.
The Royal Family waits alone.
Now television cameras whirr
Like cats at last induced to purr.

You know those moments that there are
When, lonely under moon and star,
You wait upon a beach?
Suddenly all Creation's near
And complicated things are clear,
Eternity in reach!
So we who watch the action done –
A mother to her kneeling son
The Crown of office giving –
Can hardly tell, so rapt our gaze
Whether but seconds pass or days
Or in what age we're living.

You knelt a boy, you rose a man.
And thus your lonelier life began.

In 1936 or thereabouts my wife and I used to get great pleasure from an anthology of passages from letters written to E. V. Lucas, in a book he edited called *Post-Bag Diversions* – particularly from the only one not in fact written to him, but written by a young girl to her aunt. The War came, and we moved, and the book disappeared, and it took me fifty years to find it again. But it turned up at last a few months ago, and, turning to the letter, we got as much pleasure from it as we had done before. Unfortunately Lucas doesn't tell us the name of the girl, or the date of writing.

Letter from a Girl to Her Aunt Telling of a Remarkable Experience at a Dinner Party:
from 'Post-Bag Diversions' edited by E. V. LUCAS

I went in to dinner with a very shy young man – rather pretty he was, with a fair moustache. I made a very bad beginning because I took hold of the back of my chair and the top came off in my hand just as Mr Smith was beginning to say grace, and it so upset me that I dropped my roll straight into my soup with a splash. Then I couldn't make out the young man at all. He talked a great deal of slang but he didn't seem to want to take a ticket for our café chantant and he said he never danced, but I never thought he was a parson because of his ordinary evening dress and his moustache.

Then a terrible drama began. We were eating mince-pies and I suddenly looked and beheld Daddy tethered by a string leading from his mouth to the middle of the table. A bit of the table centre had frayed, a string had crossed his plate and Daddy had eaten the end with his mince-pie. I felt the shy young man was talking to me but I never heard a word he said, and I caught Mum's eye who was opposite. She saw it too and began to grow redder and redder . . .

Daddy in blissful ignorance was talking blithely to his neighbour and chewing mince-pie and string. Then he moved his head and the string caught the wine-glasses. They wobbled about; he looked rather worried – put them straight – and then of course they wobbled again. At last he began to think something was going wrong so he put a large piece of mince-pie out of his mouth and on to his plate and all was well. Then the maid took Daddy's plate away and the portion of mince-pie remained behind! It sat on the table in front of him. Mum and I were going through gymnastic feats to keep our faces straight. She was simply red in the face and the tears began to run down my cheeks. Then my dear Papa, still being blind to the awful situation, knocked the piece of mince-pie off the table on to his knee, thereby pulling the string so that a portion of the table centre jumped forward and the glasses hopped about. Then he continued his conversation and Mum and I were just beginning to calm down a bit when he suddenly pushed the table centre back and up flew the bit of mince-pie off his knee on to the table with a wild hop that nearly finished Mum and me off . . .

Finally I believe he cut the string but before that happened I was roused by the shy young man repeating over and over again: 'I don't know why you should laugh, I am sure. I shouldn't say I was a curate if I wasn't. I don't see why it's so funny.' All the time he was explaining he was a curate at St Thomas's I never heard a word. I was reduced to mopping my tears with my dinner-napkin and giving dreadful and unexpected gurgles and the more I tried to explain that I wasn't laughing at him the more certain he got that I was – so it never got settled at all. And Daddy never knew till we told him all about it driving home.

Readers: Sarah Badel, Christopher Fry

Full Selection:
Pilgrim's Progress, JOHN BUNYAN
Ode on the Death of the Duke of Wellington, ALFRED, LORD TENNYSON
Love's Caution, W. H. DAVIES
Extract from a Letter to Her Publisher, SYLVIA TOWNSEND WARNER
Retired Cat, WILLIAM COWPER
The Naming of Cats, T. S. ELIOT
The Naming of Parts, HENRY REED
Little Dorrit, CHARLES DICKENS
The Purple Land, W. H. HUDSON
How in Heaven's Name Did Columbus Get Over, ARTHUR HUGH CLOUGH
Lord Jim, JOSEPH CONRAD
Frederick the Great, THOMAS MANN
Ballad of the Investiture 1969, JOHN BETJEMAN
The Mayor of Casterbridge, THOMAS HARDY
The Later Years of Thomas' Hardy, F. E. HARDY
A Luncheon, MAX BEERBOHM
Letter from a Girl to Her Aunt Telling of a Remarkable Experience at a Dinner Party (From 'Post Bag Diversions' edited by E. V. Lucas)
Divine Poems XIV, JOHN DONNE
Ecclesiastes, 12

PROFESSOR
ALAN GEMMELL

1982

As a newly graduated botanist, Alan Gemmell applied for a Common-wealth Fellowship to the United States. When asked what sort of research he intended to do there, he replied 'I want to research on improving golf course greens.' A far cry, perhaps, from presenting 'Gardeners' Question Time', but it is a clear example of the good humour that has entertained millions of listeners through the years. The story of how he got that job too is told below. His account of how he made his choice for 'With Great Pleasure' is perhaps the most convincing of many I have read. 'Why they gave me pleasure I'm not awfully sure in some cases. In some I'm absolutely certain. In others I can rationalise and make up reasons why I like them, but some others I just like because they are. And I think always it's a mistake to look for inwardness in everything; simplicity is a virtue in itself.'

Anybody who has been born in Glasgow – you can only be born in Glasgow once – always has a deep sentimental attachment to it. It is such a jolly, dirty, rough, drunken city, but it is full of a very kind set of people with a language of their own. If you listen to an interview of streetmen – passers-by in Glasgow streets – they need translating, half of them. And Glasgow has a sense of humour all its own. There are only two cities to my mind in Britain which one recognises as having real personalities. One is Glasgow and the other is Liverpool. They both are jolly, they both are dirty, but they have a warmth and humour about them which transcends the apparent disadvantages which physically they might suffer from.

To find a quotation about Glasgow is easy because there are lots of books which stress the rather dirty side of Glasgow, but I'd like to offer you an extract from a book called *Dancing in the Streets* by a tiny little man called Clifford Hanley, which explains one side of Glasgow life beautifully.

That Music Stuff
CLIFFORD HANLEY

There is always a lot of singing in Glasgow, everybody does it. Burns songs, pop songs, folk songs, operatic songs, patriotic songs, all kinds of songs. But mostly, in terms of sheer bulk, passionately sentimental songs.

Every wedding in Glasgow proves that every family in Glasgow has at least one singing uncle, usually called Willie. The Uncle Willies tend to choose songs with a bit of tone, like 'Red, Red Rose', or the 'Rowan Tree'. Both of these are certain death to amateur singers, but they die happy and proud. They take pride in a good-going tremolo, produce very rolling r's, very broad a's, and o's and u's so narrow you could slice a cheese with them, and whatever the tempo, when they hit a good note fair and square, they hang on to it till they've milked it of every drop of passion.

Singing is not permitted by law in Glasgow pubs, because Glasgow understands the dangerous power of music, which inflames as readily as it soothes; especially as pub singers would always be liable to come up with 'The Wild Colonial Boy', or 'Ra Sash my Farra Wore', either of them guaranteed to spark off a crusade.

But buskers sing outside the pubs, and customers sing after they leave the pubs. They still cling to their ancient favourites, for instance:

> 'Ra pale mune wos raaaaaaaaaaaaaaaa-ising,
> Above rgrnmounte-e-e-e-e-e-e-ens . . .'

Or the song that is the Glasgow drunkard's national anthem, although Glasgow (and Will Fyffe) gave the rest of the world 'I belong to Glasgow' for the world's drinking parties. But

Glasgow's own choice is 'The Bonnie Wells o' Wearie', pronounced 'Rab Onie Wells a Wee-a-rie'. Glaswegians never sing this song sober because it is believed to bring on rain.

I left Glasgow and moved to live in the west coast town of Troon. In school we learnt a verse of poetry every night. We had to recite it the next day. You could walk round the school and through the windows of the classrooms you'd hear 'Gray's Elegy' being done, the curfew was tolling the knell in 4b or whatever it was. The main town on the west coast of Scotland, in my mind, is always Ayr, and I went to Ayr Academy, founded in the thirteenth century, a school with an enormous sense of tradition and history. The Romans were in Ayr, Wallace and Bruce started the wars against the English in Ayr. In fact, the only history I ever learnt was Scots history. I couldn't tell you the name of a single King or Queen of England apart from Edward the First because Scotland beat him at the battle of Bannockburn. But in Ayr there was another thing – Burns was born just outside Ayr. We were made to learn and got to like and love his poetry. He's difficult in some of his things, but to my mind he's the best lyric poet writer I've ever met. Practically all his words are monosyllables, and yet they convey thoughts that are very lovely, very deep. And one of the simplest and best is the one that Cliff Hanley mentioned.

A Red, Red Rose
ROBERT BURNS

> O my Luve's like a red, red rose,
>   That's newly sprung in June;
> O my Luve's like the melodie
> That's sweetly played in tune.
>
> As Fair art thou, my bonie lass,
>   So deep in luve am I;
> And I will love thee still, my Dear,
>   Till a' the seas gang dry.
>
> Till a' the seas gang dry, my Dear,
>   And the rocks melt wi' the sun;
> O I will love thee still, my Dear,
>   While the sands o' life shall run.

And fare thee weel, my only Luve!
And fare thee weel, a while!
And I will come again, my Luve,
Tho' it were ten thousand mile!

When I went up to the University at Glasgow, I went up with the
full intention of reading Honours Chemistry and becoming a
school teacher. But across the road from us in Troon there lived a
man called Daniel Grant O'Brien to whom I've always been
grateful. He was an agriculturalist who worked in the Agricul-
tural College at Auchincruive near Ayr who one day said to my
mother, 'If Alan can get a good degree in Botany, I can get him a
job.' This was at the time of the Depression, so when I came home
from the University one day my mother met me at the door and
said, 'You're not a chemist any more, you're a botanist.' When I
was a boy at school I had always thought of Botany as a terribly
feminine occupation, that it was to do with gathering flowers,
that it was to do with everything that was gentle and Victorian.
But then I got an interest in Natural History and I started reading
Gilbert White. He wrote *The Natural History of Selborne* in 1788. He
writes a lot about birds, but in one letter he writes to the
Honourable Daines Barrington about botany, and it was this that
made me decide to accept my mother's command. I had little
option.

Letter to The Honourable Daines Barrington from *Natural History and Antiquities of Selborne*
GILBERT WHITE

The standing objection to botany has always been, that it is a
pursuit that amuses the fancy and exercises the memory, without
improving the mind or advancing any real knowledge: and,
where the science is carried no farther than a mere systematic
classification, the charge is but too true. But the botanist that is
desirous of wiping off this aspersion should be by no means
content with a list of names, he should study plants philosophi-
cally, should investigate the laws of vegetation, should examine
the powers and virtues of efficacious herbs, should promote their
cultivation; and graft the gardener, the planter, and the husbandman, on the phytologist. Not that system is by any means to be

thrown aside; without system the field of Nature would be a pathless wilderness: but system should be subservient to, not the main object of, pursuit.

Instead of examining the minute distinctions of every various species of obscure genus, the botanist should endeavour to make himself acquainted with those that are useful. You shall see a man readily ascertain every herb of the field, yet hardly know wheat from barley, or at least one sort of wheat or barley from another.

But of all sorts of vegetation the grasses seem to be most neglected; neither the farmer nor the grazier seem to distinguish the annual from the perennial, the hardy from the tender, nor the succulent and nutritive from the dry and juiceless.

The study of grasses would be of great consequence to a northerly and grazing kingdom. The botanist that could improve the sward of the district where he lived would be a useful member of society: to raise a thick turf on a naked soil would be worth volumes of systematic knowledge; and he would be the best commonwealth's man that could occasion the growth of 'two blades of grass where only one was seen before'.

Every gardener starts as a reluctant gardener and I did this. My father bade me do it, and being a dutiful obedient son, I half did it. But I've got to like it. After a bit of wandering I ended up in Manchester, at the University there, where I was a lecturer in the Botany Department. A fellow lecturer in the Botany Department, a man called Samson, was a charming man who smoked a pipe; he always knocked it out in the palm of his hands and then rubbed his hands over his face and by half past nine in the morning he had black stripes down his face. I remember him meeting me in the corridor one day and saying to me in all seriousness, 'You know, Alan, what's wrong with this University is that there are no eccentrics in it.' And there he was . . . But Samson was a very good botanist, especially a horticultural botanist, and he had been asked to participate in a new gardening programme that was starting in Manchester in 1947. He had participated in it for about a couple of years and then, probably thanks to his face, he was appointed to a chair of Botany in the University of Ebaden in West Africa. He was asked if he could suggest somebody who might replace him in 'Gardeners'

Question Time'. Now Samson was a Scotsman, and if you ask a Scotsman a question like that he's not going to suggest a Welshman or an Englishman, so he said, 'Now, there's a tall, handsome, dark-haired young man in the Department called Gemmell, try him.' So I started in 1949. And because it's been such a major part of life, I wondered what bit about gardening gave me the most pleasure, and I thought of the poems, as you all will do, about daffodils and daisies and 'Bavarian Gentians' and poems like that, and decided no, I won't have that. What I will have is an essay which was written by Francis Bacon in 1625 about gardens.

The Moral and Historical Works of Lord Bacon
Chapter XLVI – of Gardens
FRANCIS BACON

God Almighty first planted a garden; and, indeed, it is the purest of human pleasures; it is the greatest refreshment to the spirits of man; without which buildings and palaces are but gross handy-works; and as man shall ever see, that, when ages grow to civility and elegancy, men come to build stately, sooner than to garden finely; as if gardening were the greater perfection. I do hold it in the royal ordering òf gardens, there ought to be gardens for all months in the year, in which, severally, things of beauty may be then in season.

And because the breath of flowers is far sweeter in the air (where it comes and goes, like the warbling of music), than in the hand, therefore nothing is more fit for that delight, than to know what be the flowers and plants that do best perfume the air. Roses, damask and red, are fast flowers of their smells; so that you may walk by a whole row of them, and find nothing of their sweetness; yea, though it be in a morning's dew. Bays, likewise, yield no smell as they grow, rosemary little, nor sweet marjoram; that which, above all others, yields the sweetest smell in the air, is the violet, especially the white double violet, which comes twice a year, about the middle of April, and about Bartholomew-tide. Next to that is the musk-rose; then the strawberry-leaves dying, with a most excellent cordial smell; then the flower of the vines, it is a little dust like the dust of a bent, which grows upon the cluster in the first coming forth; then the sweet-briar then wallflowers, which are very delightful to be set under a parlour or lower chamber window; then pinks and gilliflower; then the flowers of the lime-tree; then the honeysuckles, so they be somewhat afar off. Of bean-flowers I speak not, because they are field flowers; but those which perfume the air most delightfully, not passed by as the rest, but being trodden upon and crushed, are three; that is, burnet, wild thyme, and water-mints; therefore you are to set whole alleys of them, to have the pleasure when you walk or tread.

I've often wondered, because I was trained as a scientist, and have lived all my life as a scientist really, what is the peculiar attraction of gardens – why so many people do, and enjoy, gardening. I think it's a combination of a number of things: First of all it gives very ordinary people the power to create something that's beautiful out of bare soil. For those that are sedentary, it gives them physical exercise if they'll take advantage of it. It also has a marvellous thing about it that somehow or other, your mistakes in gardening are never permanent – if the thing dies you can try it again next year, in the same or in a different place, a different variety, you can plant it at a different time. Finally – I don't know if it's a combination of all these or if it's something quite different – constant working in the garden gives you what I hate to call 'a peace and a philosophy and a kind of mystic communion', which sounds terribly twee, but undoubtedly is true. This feeling about gardens is not mine alone – it's very very many people's and it was expressed in a dialogue which was written by Ralph Austen in 1676. It's a dialogue between the husbandman and the fruit trees in the orchard.

A Dialogue Between the Husbandman and Fruit-trees
RALPH AUSTEN

HUSBANDMAN.   Methinks ye swagger and are very brave this May morning, in your beautiful blossoms and green leaves. Whence had ye all this gallantry?
FRUIT-TREES.   It pleased our bountiful Creator to bestow it upon us; but it is for thee, and for the sake of mankind which engageth thee, and all men, to acknowledge it, and to serve Him and praise Him with more cheerfulness. This is our language and

lesson to all men, which every particular tree among us does daily speak aloud.

HUSBANDMAN. Ye have many visitors, frequently. Have you this familiar discourse with every one as we have at present, and as often as we are disposed?

FRUIT-TREES. Many people, of all sorts, come from time to time, and walk among us, and look upon us, and commend us for brave handsome trees, lovely and beautiful, especially when we are in our gallantries, full of beautiful blossoms and pleasant and wholesome fruits; and some greedily pluck us, and tear us, and sometimes break off some of our branches to get our fruits, and so go on their ways, but never speak a word with us, neither do they understand what we say to them . . .

HUSBANDMAN. Come, my friends, let us walk into this pleasant garden and have some further discourse with those innocent, harmless companions, the fruit-trees. They will bid us welcome and are still ready and at leisure to confer with us . . . But we must not forget what hath often been said concerning the way and the manner of their discourse with men: that it is not audible to the outward sense of hearing, in the sound of words, but always to the inward sense, the mind and understanding.

Scientists are thought to be strange people, and in many ways they are. And as a biologist, of course, I am a scientist, and science, especially biology, is a very rewarding exercise. You have the pleasure of doing experiments, you have the pleasure of explaining to people, you have a lot of frustration, but there's great happiness in it. Unfortunately scientists tend to be looked on by many of the population as people who are terribly hard, terribly based on material things, terribly rigid with little imagination. Having said that, probably the greatest biological scientist who ever lived was Darwin. He has been having a very bad press recently. He published his *Origin of Species*, in which he propounded his theory of evolution by natural selection, in 1859, and for a theory in science to last that length of time is not bad. In fact it's very good. Although his theory can be criticised and although Darwin can be criticised in many things, much of the criticism springs from the fact that he couldn't be expected to have had the knowledge then that we have now. It comes too from people who have never read his works and who have never really tried to understand them, and none of the critics has ever produced a theory which will match and encompass the things that the theory of evolution does.

But Darwin's publication started off an enormous religious controversy: people who believed in Darwin and thought Darwin was probably correct were tarred with a brush as being unfeeling, atheistic, unthinking clods.

If you read Darwin, you'll find a charm, you'll find a simplicity, you'll find a beauty of expression and you'll find a depth of feeling that somehow or other never gets into the ordinary conversation, and that's why I've chosen to end this selection of things I like with the last paragraph of *Origin of Species*.

Origin of Species
CHARLES DARWIN

It is interesting to contemplate an entangled bank, clothed with many plants of many kinds, with birds singing on the bushes, with various insects flitting about, and with worms crawling through the damp earth, and to reflect that these elaborately constructed forms, so different from each other, and dependent on each other in so complex a manner, have all been produced by laws acting around us. These laws, taken in the largest sense, being Growth and Reproduction; Inheritence which is almost implied by reproduction; Variability from the indirect and direct action of the external conditions of life, and from use and disuse; a Ratio of Increase so high as to lead to a Struggle for Life, and as a consequence to Natural Selection, entailing Divergence of Character and the Extinction of less-improved forms. Thus, from the war of nature, from famine and death, the most exalted object which we are capable of conceiving, namely the production of the higher animals, directly follows. There is a grandeur in this view of life, with its several powers, having been originally breathed into a few forms or into one; and that, whilst this planet has gone cycling on according to the fixed law of gravity, from so simple a beginning endless forms most beautiful and most wonderful have been, and are being, evolved.

Readers: Douglas Blackwell, John Cairney

Full Selection:
Disenchantment, C. E. MONTAGUE
That Music Stuff, from *Dancing in the Streets* CLIFFORD HANLEY
A Red, Red Rose, ROBERT BURNS
Seaside Golf, JOHN BETJEMAN
Letter to The Honourable Daines Barrington, GILBERT WHITE
A Drink with Something in It, OGDEN NASH
Prospice, ROBERT BROWNING
The Moral and Historical Works of Lord Bacon: XLVI
A Dialogue Between the Husbandman and Fruit-trees, RALPH AUSTEN
The Spring Was Late that Year, VITA SACKVILLE-WEST
When You Are Old, W. B. YEATS
Origin of Species, CHARLES DARWIN

RICHARD GORDON

1979

Medical fiction, hospital romances featuring stern-jawed doctors/special-ists/anaesthetists/ and patients heroic in suffering, or wise old fellows in country practices and so on, have long been queue-jumpers in the best-seller lists. Doctor Richard Gordon's novels detailing some of the comic horror inherent in the day-to-day life of the medical profession came as a refreshing incision into the pulp. But wonderfully funny and entertaining though they were, he has been careful not to spend a lifetime merely churning out the same sort of stuff. Just as Dirk Bogarde, who starred so elegantly in Doctor in the House *and other 'Doctor' films, went on to become a fine and subtle actor in a variety of character roles, so Gordon has written stronger, more serious novels,*

*many with a medical background, to be sure, but which dig deeper
into the personalities of the people he created. To the delight of the
listeners, however, his selection for 'With Great Pleasure', recorded at
St Bartholomew's Hospital, was chosen entirely with laughter in
mind.*

I became a novelist entirely by mistake. I had got a job on the
British Medical Journal. I went along there with the idea of
starting a doctor's comic column, but the editor having a rather
sharper sense of humour than I had, put me in charge of the
Obituary Notices. I always claim that this was invaluable practice
– it taught me how to write convincing fiction. Well unfortunately
one week I killed a Doctor of Divinity by mistake. I won't bore you
with the details, but it became necessary to put as much space
between myself and the British Medical Journal as possible, so I
ran away to sea – in comfort. I signed on as a ship's doctor aboard
a cargo boat sailing from London to Australia. Now nobody told
me before we started that we were going via Newfoundland,
which is rather a long way round, you must admit. I mean
I wondered what all those icebergs were doing all over the
place, and either I had the healthiest crew who'd ever sailed the
seven seas or else they distrusted the look of me, because I never
had a patient, not a single one. I'd nothing to do all day
except drink whisky with the chief engineer and listen to his
stories about Glasgow, because all chief engineers come from
Glasgow. It was really as a public health measure, to prevent
myself getting cirrhosis of the liver, that when we got to the
Tropics I put up a typewriter in a shady corner of the deck and
I started writing about my experiences at Barts as a medical
student. I intended the book to be a cross between *War and Peace*
and *Gray's Anatomy*, but somehow it didn't turn out like that at
all.

Medical students seem heartless, or they make themselves
seem so, but of course that's only half the story. I think it was best
put by John Brown, a nineteenth-century doctor/writer living in
Edinburgh, who wrote about medical students in his book *Rab
and his Friends*.

Rab and His Friends
JOHN BROWN

Don't think (medical students) heartless; they are neither better nor worse than you or I: they get over their professional horrors, and into their proper work; and in them pity as an *emotion* ending in itself or at best in tears and a long-drawn breath, lessens, while pity, as a *motive*, is quickened, and gains power and purpose. It is well for poor human nature that it is so.

I think that explains why many of us take up medicine.

It is perhaps appropriate that I should write *Doctor in the House* on the way to Canada because one of my favourite authors was Stephen Leacock. He was a very comic writer who was a Professor of Economics at McGill University and he also wrote serious books. I've also written serious books, I've recently written *The Private Life of Florence Nightingale*, so I can sympathise with Stephen Leacock when a lady told him she'd read all the way through his *Principles of Economics* roaring her head off at every page, but here is his most accurate description of how to be a doctor.

How to Be a Doctor
STEPHEN LEACOCK

'What about diet, doctor?' says the patient, completely cowed.

The answer to this question varies very much. It depends on how the doctor is feeling and whether it is long since he had a meal himself. If it is late in the morning and the doctor is ravenously hungry, he says:

'Oh, eat plenty, don't be afraid of it; eat meat, vegetables, starch, glue, cement, anything you like.' But if the doctor has just had lunch and if his breathing is short-circuited with huckleberry pie, he says very firmly:

'No, I don't want you to eat anything at all: absolutely not a bite; it won't hurt you, a little self-denial in the matter of eating is the best thing in the world.'

'And what about drinking?' Again the doctor's answer varies. He may say:

'Oh, yes, you might drink a glass of lager now and then, or, if you prefer it, a gin and soda or a whisky and Apollinaris, and I think before going to bed I'd take a hot Scotch with a couple of lumps of white sugar and a bit of lemon-peel in it and a good grating of nutmeg on the top.' The doctor says this with real feeling, and his eye glistens with the pure love of his profession. But if, on the other hand, the doctor has spent the night before at a little gathering of medical friends, he is very apt to forbid the patient to touch alcohol in any shape, and to dismiss the subject with great severity.

I don't suppose any of you have read any of my books, at least I hope not because I think the only people who read my books are people who are ill in hospital. I know this for a fact because a lady told me at a literary lunch the other day, over the trifle – she was wearing a lovely hat which matched it – 'Oh,' she said, 'my husband did so enjoy your latest novel. Such a pity he died when he was half way through.' Well, I think she was quite right, the best part of the book was the ending. But if you haven't read any of my books, I do hope you've seen some of the 'Doctor' films; you can still see them on television if you stay up late enough at night. If you have seen them I shall be terribly hurt if you haven't noticed that I have a small part in each of them. In the first one I played the anaesthetist. That was type-casting because when I was a doctor at Barts I *was* an anaesthetist, and now I can reveal to you why I became an anaesthetist: I couldn't stand talking to my patients. For an anaesthetist, you see, it's easy; you come in: 'Good morning,' needle in, bang, out flat. If I had taken my career very seriously I would have become a pathologist and then the patients would have been even less trouble!

Of course I'm only one of very many doctors who've made the transition into writing. To mention just a few: Tobias Smollett, a naval surgeon, who wrote *Roderick Random*; Oliver Goldsmith; Oliver Wendell Holmes; John Keats – Guy's man I'm afraid – he died at the age of twenty-six from tuberculosis. Conan Doyle was a doctor who based his famous Sherlock Holmes on Dr Bell who taught him in Edinburgh; A. J. Cronin whom one knows; Robert Bridges, the poet – a Barts man I'm glad to say; and of course Somerset Maugham. Right to the end of his long life he remained, like myself, on the Medical Register, and, like myself, was presumably perfectly entitled to write prescriptions for dangerous drugs or deliver a baby, had the occasion arisen and had he happened to feel like it.

I've also found, apart from those writers, twelve medical pirates. I am referring of course to the sea-going and not the Harley Street variety, and ten medical murderers – those of course were the ones who were found out. These include Dr Palmer, who was one of the last men to be hanged in public in this country – he was certainly the last doctor to be hanged in this country in public – outside Stafford Gaol on a very wet morning in 1856. He had killed his family and thirteen other people with strychnine which must have been very painful, and I'm sorry to say that Dr Palmer was a Barts man. Of course here at Barts we're all rather sensitive about the good doctor's end, so we explain that he was attending an open air meeting in an important capacity when the platform unfortunately collapsed beneath his feet.

Well now I'm going to confess something to you. I see medicine these days only as a patient. I suffer from gout. It's a thankless disease to have; most diseases attract sympathy, gout attracts only derision. One of my nicest friends used to hit me on the back and say, 'Ah, gout. Got your nose too deep into the port, old boy, what?' And I'm afraid that port and gout are linked in the public mind as firmly and as erroneously as wet feet and a cold in the head, or sitting on stones gives you piles. The poet William Cowper in 1782 wrote quite slanderously:

> Pangs arthritic that infest the toe
> Of libertine excess.

It's a very literary disease, but it is due not to port, but to purines. A. P. Herbert wrote in *Punch*:

> At last the happy truth is out –
> Port wine is *not* the cause of gout;
> Far more responsible for pain
> Are kidneys, liver, sweetbread, brain –
> The clubman should by any means
> Avoid anchovies and sardines,
> And citizens of every sort
> Owe some apology to port!

I think I must also quote Sir Thomas Browne, the seventeenth-century physician and author, about gout:

What famous men, what emperors and learned persons have been severe examples of that disease, and that it is not a disease of fools, but of men of parts and senses.

Many modern doctors say the same, but only, I think, because they've got gout themselves.

Reader: Dinsdale Landen

Full Selection:
The Pickwick Papers, CHARLES DICKENS
Rab and His Friends, JOHN BROWN
How to Be a Doctor, STEPHEN LEACOCK
The Diary of a Nobody, GEORGE and WEEDON GROSSMITH
1066 and All That, SELLARS and YEATMAN
England, Their England, A. G. MACDONNEL
Right Ho, Jeeves, P. G. WODEHOUSE
Pangs Arthritic, WILLIAM COWPER
At Last the Happy Truth Is Out, A. P. HERBERT
On Gout, SIR THOMAS BROWNE
Old Man's Wish, WALTER POPE

GENERAL
SIR JOHN HACKETT

1971

Sir John's programme tells a story of an escape, or to be more accurate two escapes. The first is from a hospital behind enemy lines during the last war, a long, painful, dangerous escape which involved his being kept in hiding while his wounds healed. The second escape was an escape of the mind from pain and boredom, an escape provided by literature. It is a tribute to Sir John's account of that second escape – 'It is a great pleasure to me to be allowed to talk about a chapter in my life, only a few months long, which unfolded before most of you were born' – that it seems as filled with drama and adventure as the first.

In the Autumn of 1944 I was commanding a brigade of around a thousand parachute infantry and jumped with them in the First British Airborne Division in the battle near Arnhem by which we hoped to seize and hold the crossing of the lower Rhine. We had ammunition, food and everything else for two or three days, until ground forces should come up to us. They never came and after eight days of hard fighting the remnant of the First Airborne Division – two thousand men out of ten thousand – were withdrawn back across the river Rhine, leaving the badly wounded behind in the hands of the enemy.

I was one of these, with severe wounds in the stomach from a shell splinter and a bullet through the thigh. Only a surgical miracle, as I have heard it described, performed by one of our own surgeons, kept me alive. Ten days after that surgeon had taken the splinter out and sewn my insides together again, the

Dutch Underground smuggled me through the SS guard out of the hospital and brought me to a township a few miles from Arnhem along the Utrecht road. That was how I came into the care of four middle-aged sisters and the son and daughter of one of them, in a little house set back in its garden a few yards from the street, less than thirty yards away from a German military police billet next door.

That was the start of the adventure in poetry I now have it in mind to talk about.

It was into an attic bedroom in this small, old-fashioned house that I was carried, by now absolutely all in, one night in late October 1944, and put to bed under a sampler embroidered with a scene from the Sleeping Beauty with the text (in Dutch), 'And she slept for a hundred years'. I never read anything more welcome.

One of the four middle-aged sisters who were hiding me from the Germans, had been in England and had trained there to teach English. In a day or two, when I was a little restored, this one, Aunt Ann, brought me her books. They included the Authorised Version of the Bible, the Oxford editions of Wordsworth and of Scott's verse, a complete *Oxford Shakespeare* in one volume and a book called *One Thousand and One Gems of English Verse*, edited by one Charles McKay.

Books to read in English! This was providential! But reflection upon the situation in which I found myself induced no great inclination to look for reading which gave an echo to it. The world outside our house in Torenstraat was full of unseen menace. When I was able to move to the window and look out I could see soldiers of the enemy walking unsuspecting in the street, always armed and often ludicrously young. In the mornings I would sometimes hear them marching and listened while they sang. This was not as British infantry soldiers used to sing as they marched, full throated and cynical and sentimental at the same time, to a swinging rhythm. What these sang was threatening, crisp and cocky, the singing voices clipped off at the end of a phrase (tramp, tramp) with another couplet sung and switched off as suddenly (tramp, tramp) as the sounds moved round the corner and down the street.

My life in this house became one of reflection, recollection and further exploration. In my little iron bed in that attic room I read the whole of Wordsworth. There was time in plenty and little to distract me. The embarrassment of choice offered by a large library did not exist here and I simply read what I had. I was now able to discover for myself that Wordsworth was a great poet. To read, for example, those two very long poems, 'The Prelude' and 'The Excursion' as continuous pieces and no longer see them only as quarries from which examination papers were hewn was a revelation. I even did what I had never dreamt of doing before and read through those almost endless sonnet sequences, mostly about the Established Church. There were other small things I was glad to see again – the sonnet on the sonnet for example.

The Uses and Beauties of the Sonnet
WILLIAM WORDSWORTH

Nuns fret not at their convent's narrow room;
And hermits are contented with their cells;
And students with their pensive citadels;
Maids at the wheel, the weaver at his loom,
Sit blithe and happy; bees that soar for bloom,
High as the highest peak of Furness Fells,
Will murmur by the hour in foxglove bells;
In truth, the prison, unto which we doom
Ourselves, no prison is: and hence to me,
In sundry moods, 'twas pastime to be bound
Within the Sonnet's scanty plot of ground:
Pleased if some souls (for such there needs must be)
Who have felt the weight of too much liberty,
Should find brief solace there, as I have found.

I doubt if many of you who are students think of yourselves as living in 'pensive citadels'. But in the enclosed and inward turning life I lived just then it was to me most apt. Beautiful words too in spite of so much sibilance. It had been Tennyson, I seemed to recall, who spoke of getting rid of too many S-sounds as 'kicking the geese out of the boat'. But 'pensive citadels' was lovely, to be lingered over and added to remembered sounds like 'pavement' and 'cellar door' as a source of quiet pleasure. I now found more within the ordered framework of the sonnet than ever before.

I could read things that pleased or helped me again and again, for there was no hurry. I could find, and enjoy, comparisons. There was Eliza Cook's 'The Old Arm Chair', for example, typical of a certain time and of a literary outlook prevalent then but not easy to share now.

The Old Arm Chair
ELIZA COOK

I love it – I love it, and who shall dare
To chide me for loving that old arm chair!
I've treasured it long as a sainted prize –
I've bedewed it with tears, and embalmed it with sighs;
'Tis bound by a thousand bands to my heart,
Not a tie will break, not a link will start.
Would you learn the spell? a mother sat there;
And a sacred thing is that old arm chair.

In childhood's hour I lingered near
The hallowed seat with listening ear;
And gentle words that mother would give,
To fit me to die, and teach me to live.
She told me shame would never betide,
With truth for my creed and God for my guide;
She taught me to lisp my earliest prayer,
As I knelt beside that old arm chair.

I sat and watched her many a day,
When her eyes grew dim and her locks were grey,
And I almost worshipped her when she smiled
And turned from her Bible to bless her child.
Years rolled on, but the last one sped –
My idol was shattered – my earth star fled:
I learnt how much the heart can bear,
When I saw her die in that old arm chair.

'Tis past! 'tis past! but I gaze on it now
With quivering breath and throbbing brow:
'Twas there she nursed me – 'twas there she died,

And memory flows with lava tide –
Say it is folly, and deem me weak,
While the scalding tears run down my cheek.
But I love it – I love it, and cannot tear
My soul from my mother's old arm chair.

I compared that Victorian sentimentality with the truer sentiment of those lines of Cowper, on a mother's picture.

On the Receipt of a Mother's Picture
WILLIAM COWPER

O that those lips had language! Life has pass'd
   With me but roughly since I heard thee last.
Those lips are thine – thy own sweet smiles I see,
   The same, that oft in childhood solac'd me;
Voice only fails, else how distinct they say,
   'Grieve not, my child, chase all thy fears away!'
The meek intelligence of those dear eyes
   (Blest be the art that can immortalise,
The art that baffles Time's tyrannic claim
   To quench it) here shines on me still the same.

Faithful remembrancer of one so dear,
   O welcome guest, though unexpected here!
Who bidd'st me honor with an artless song,
   Affectionate, a mother lost so long,
I will obey, not willingly alone,
   But gladly, as the precept were her own:
And, while that face renewed my filial grief,
   Fancy shall weave a charm for my relief,
Shall steep me in Elysian reverie,
   A momentary dream, that thou art she.

A young Dutch minister of the Reformed Church was brought to see me secretly. This was Dominie Blauw, brave pastor of a harassed flock, one of very few allowed by the ladies of this house to know that I was there. He lent me at my request St Matthew in Greek.

As autumn moved on towards winter the Dutch Underground was busy planning my escape. I had hoped to be at home in

England for Christmas, but in mid-December I could still scarcely walk. Such a liability for any party trying to make its hazardous way through the German lines would be intolerable and I made them leave me out of their plans. One party of escapers from the Airbornes did in fact get through. Another failed and after that German security tightened up so hard in that sensitive area just north of the lower Rhine near Arnhem that we could only hope for later opportunities elsewhere.

I could see out of the window from my bed the branches of a tree waving in the autumn winds. Its leaves had gone – all but one, which stayed a long time alone on the bare branch until one day I awoke and saw that it had gone too. This seemed to me a sign that I knew I must accept.

It was then that I rediscovered Milton.

On His Blindness
JOHN MILTON

> When I consider how my light is spent
> Ere half my days in this dark world and wide,
> And that one talent which is death to hide,
> Lodg'd with me useless, though my Soul more bent
> To serve therewith my Maker, and present
> My true account, lest he returning chide;
> Doth God exact day-labour, light deny'd,
> I fondly ask; but patience to prevent
> That murmur, soon replies, 'God doth not need
> Either man's work or his own gifts; who best
> Bear his mild yoke, they serve him best: his state
> Is kingly: thousands at his bidding speed,
> And post o'er land and ocean without rest;
> They also serve who only stand and wait'.

I read that over and over again. I re-read 'Lycidas' and thought of many friends now gone. 'For Lycidas is dead, dead ere his prime, Young Lycidas and hath not left his peer.' I rediscovered old acquaintance in 'Il Penseroso' and the pleasures of Melancholy, and in 'L'Allegro', which banishes it in pretty round terms 'Hence loathèd Melancholy, of Cerberus and blackest midnight born, in

Stygian Cave forlorn, 'mongst horrid shapes and shrieks and sights unholy . . .'

But I now began to develop a longing for one great whole work above all others. It all began with the 'Gems'. It was fed by what I read in any other books I had. It was nourished by recollection and reflection. What I wanted above all was *Paradise Lost*. I wanted the whole of it. The 'Gems' only contained parts – long enough to leave one tuned in to the rhythm and the language and the images but frustrated at having to stop.

After four months I got away, piloted on a borrowed bicycle by a young friend, John Snoek, through snowy landscapes like a winter scene of Brueghel, with faultlessly forged papers and on my coat a little button of a type well known there, proclaiming that I was hard of hearing. I journeyed from one underground hideout to another. We were taken over the lower Rhine where the swift winter stream flowed between broken ice piled high against the banks, by a ferryman in danger of his life for putting out a boat, but unable to resist the price John offered him – a priceless skein of darning wool saved from his mother's shop. Then again in hiding until we could find more boatmen and a canoe for a journey by night through the huge marshland of the river Waal and down towards its mouth to where the southern bank was at last in allied hands. I was soon in England and they put me into a hospital to be tidied up. But when the village near Arnhem where I had lived was at last free from the enemy, I was allowed out of hospital, and the RAF lent me a little aeroplane called an Oxford, which we filled with tea and boots and chocolate and darning wool and the set of books Dominie Blauw wanted for his Doctorate in Theology, and I set off again to land for the second time in Holland.

And there my adventure story must stop. For this *is* an adventure story, I suppose. It is also a story of a poetic adventure, an experience which, in the way that a man is the product of his experience, has long been part of me. Experiences such as these are not the trimmings of life: they are part of its essential fabric and of course you do not have to get knocked about in a war to find them.

Let me only recall as we finish that my wife gave me the coming home present she had learnt I wanted most. And as I took off for

Holland for the second time I was beginning to read the whole of that majestic book that deals with 'man's first disobedience and the fruit of that forbidden tree' in such a fashion as to 'assert eternal Providence and justify the ways of God to Men'.

Readers: Sheila Allen, Julian Glover

Full Selection:
Ode on Intimations of Immortality from Recollections of Early Childhood, WILLIAM WORDSWORTH
The Uses and Beauties of the Sonnet, WILLIAM WORDSWORTH
Sonnet VIII, WILLIAM SHAKESPEARE
Sonnet X, WILLIAM SHAKESPEARE
King Lear, WILLIAM SHAKESPEARE
Quotes from the Bible
Vanity Fair, WILLIAM MAKEPIECE THACKERAY
The Rime of the Ancient Mariner, SAMUEL TAYLOR COLERIDGE
The Old Arm Chair, ELIZA COOK
On the Receipt of a Mother's Picture, WILLIAM COWPER
The Sailor's Journal, CHARLES DIBDEN
On His Blindness, JOHN MILTON
Paradise Lost, JOHN MILTON

ROY HATTERSLEY

1986

It seemed strange to be sitting in his office at the House of Commons with the Shadow Chancellor and Deputy Leader of the Labour Party and discussing not for one moment matters of urgent political debate. Indeed they were never even mentioned. Roy Hattersley was clearly more interested on this occasion in the delights of good writing. Modern British governments are not noted for their attachment to the arts, their interest, if any, boiling down in the end to a question of money and how not to spend it. It was a delight, therefore, to find such a senior politician plainly enthusiastic about literature both from the classics and from contemporary authors. We arranged to have lunch after the recording. On the day, politics did emerge briefly. Firstly the 'Daily Express' had just published an article purporting to total Hattersley's earnings and those of his wife. He was rather amused as it had apparently grossly over-estimated his and under-estimated his wife's! Then, alas, it had been decided to have Treasury matters discussed at question time so Roy was unable after all to join us for lunch. A pity as I would have enjoyed getting to know him better.

I don't support the Cruft's Dog Show school of literacy criticism which suggests that you can choose the best poem in its class and then, by comparing the champion lyric, sonnet and ballad as if they were the best Alsatian, whippet and poodle, choose a champion of champions. But if I held such views the simple and beautiful Sonnet XVIII by William Shakespeare would probably get the big rosette.

> Shall I compare thee to a Summer's day?
> Thou art more lovely and more temperate:
> Rough winds do shake the darling buds of May,
> And Summer's lease hath all too short a date:
> Sometimes too hot the eye of heaven shines,
> And often is his gold complexion dimm'd;
> And every fair from fair sometime declines,
> By chance, or nature's changing course, untrimm'd;
> But thy eternal Summer shall not fade,
> Nor lose possession of that fair thou owest;
> Nor shall Death brag thou wander'st in his shade.
> When in eternal lines to time thou growest;
>   So long as men can breathe, or eyes can see,
>   So long lives this, and this gives life to thee.

If there were such an award for prose, Lytton Strachey on the death of Queen Victoria probably qualifies.

The Passing of Victoria
GILES LYTTON STRACHEY

When, two days previously, the news of the approaching end had been made public, astonished grief had swept over the country. It appeared as if some monstrous reversal of the course of nature was about to take place. The vast majority of her subjects had never known a time when Queen Victoria had not been reigning over them. She had become an indissoluble part of their whole scheme of things, and that they were about to lose her appeared a scarcely possible thought. She herself, as she lay blind and silent, seemed to those who watched her to be divested of all thinking – to have glided already, unawares, into oblivion. Yet, perhaps, in the secret chambers of consciousness, she had her thoughts too. Perhaps her fading mind called up once more the shadows of the past to float before it, and retraced, for the last time, the vanished visions of that long history – passing back and back, through the cloud of years, to older and ever older memories – to the spring woods at Osborne, so full of primroses for Lord Beaconsfield – to Lord Palmerston's queer clothes and high demeanour, and Albert's face under the green lamp, and Albert's first stag at Balmoral, and Albert in his blue and silver uniform, and the Baron coming in through a doorway, and Lord M. dreaming at Windsor with the rooks cawing in the elm-trees, and the Archbishop of Canterbury on his knees in the dawn, and the old King's turkey-cock ejaculations, and Uncle Leopold's soft voice at Claremont, and Lehzen with the globes, and her mother's feathers sweeping down towards her, and a great old repeater-watch of her father's in its tortoise-shell case, and a yellow rug, and some friendly flounces of sprigged muslin, and the trees and the grass at Kensington.

Readers: Joss Ackland, Elizabeth Bell

Full Selection:
Sonnet XVIII, WILLIAM SHAKESPEARE
Spring and Fall, GERARD MANLEY HOPKINS
Difficult Poetry, T. S. ELIOT
Chard Whitlow, HENRY REED

American Names, STEPHEN VINCENT BENET
The Good Companions, J. B. PRIESTLEY
Removal from Terry Street, DOUGLAS DUNN
Chant-Pagan, RUDYARD KIPLING
The Passing of Victoria, GILES LYTTON STRACHEY
Dockery and Son, PHILIP LARKIN
In Memory of Eva Gore-Booth, W. B. YEATS
Into My Heart, A. E. HOUSMAN

P. D. JAMES

1985

When recording 'With Great Pleasure' we tend to avoid studios, not because there is anything wrong with them – most programmes are made in them, after all – but because much of the atmosphere of the series is due to the fact that we record in places with which the presenters have some personal connection – the town where they grew up, say, or where they settled in later life. It is also an opportunity for Radio 4 to visit a community rather than remaining cosily on its own premises. P. D. James lives in London, so we presented the programme at the New End Theatre in Hampstead, unaware that it is situated close to the radio masts for a number of minicab firms. On listening to the tapes back in Bristol, it was rather a shock to hear instructions to pick people up from dubious addresses interspersed with a stream of private jokes, along with the readings of Roy Marsden, who plays Adam Dalgliesh in the Anglia Television series of Phyllis James's novels, and Sheila Mitchell. It was some considerable time before we were able to assemble the same team in front of a different audience at the BBC's Paris Studio in Lower Regent Street!

I was educated within the State system and at one time, more than fifty years ago, I was at a school where we were required each week to learn by heart the Collect for the following Sunday. I'm not sure that it did much for my general behaviour, but how it enhanced my love of words! Today there is a risk that the majority of children will grow up ignorant of those two seminal influences in our culture, The King James Bible and the Book of Common Prayer. So here are just eighteen verses from Psalm 139 to show this deprived generation what they are missing. The psalms comprise the whole drama of humanity; birth and death, love and hate, prayer and praise, hope and fulfilment. In these verses the psalmist is contemplating the wonder of man's creation.

Psalm 139 Verses 1–18
KING JAMES VERSION

O LORD, thou hast searched me, and known me.
Thou knowest my downsitting and mine uprising,
Thou understandest my thought afar off.
Thou compassest my path and my lying down,
And art acquainted with all my ways.
For there is not a word in my tongue,
But, lo, O LORD, thou knowest it altogether.
Thou hast beset me behind and before,
And laid thine hand upon me.
Such knowledge is too wonderful for me;
It is high, I cannot attain unto it.
Whither shall I go from thy spirit?
Or whither shall I flee from thy presence?
If I ascend up into heaven, thou art there:
If I make my bed in hell, behold, thou art there.
If I take the wings of the morning,
And dwell in the uttermost parts of the sea;
Even there shall thy hand lead me,
And thy right hand shall hold me.
If I say, Surely the darkness shall cover me;
Even the night shall be light about me.
Yea, the darkness hideth not from thee;
But the night shineth as the day:

The darkness and the light are both alike to thee.
For thou hast possessed my reins:
Thou hast covered me in my mother's womb.
I will praise thee; for I am fearfully and wonderfully made:
Marvellous are thy works;
And that my soul knoweth right well.
My substance was not hid from thee,
When I was made in secret,
And curiously wrought in the lowest parts of the earth.
Thine eyes did see my substance, yet being unperfect;
And in thy book all my members were written,
Which in continuance were fashioned,
When as yet there was none of them.
How precious also are thy thoughts unto me, O God!
How great is the sum of them!
If I should count them, they are more in number than the sand:
When I awake, I am still with thee.

Poetry has been a joy to me all my life and I was fortunate in the headmaster of my primary school in Ludlow in Shropshire who loved poetry and had the gift of conveying his enthusiasm to young children. We learned a great deal by heart and recited it in the sing-song dialect of the Welsh border. Before I was eight I had kept the bridge with Horatius, defended outposts of Empire with the Gatling jammed and the Colonel dead, stood alone on the burning deck and, between these unfashionable patriotic fervours had strolled down the Shropshire lanes with A. E. Housman. It left me with a catholic taste in verse and the conviction that poetry is meant to be fun as well as wise and inspiring.

A poem which would always find a place in my personal anthology is Matthew Arnold's 'Dover Beach'. Although he lived in an age of progress and optimism, the theme of the poem and its deep pessimism seem to me more modern than Victorian. But I have always loved it, perhaps because walking by the sea is one of my keenest pleasures and this lyrical elegy on the death of faith perfectly expresses the peace, the nostalgia, the melancholy and the sense of timelessness which I experience when I look on the sea at the fading of the day.

Dover Beach
MATTHEW ARNOLD

The sea is calm to-night.
The tide is full, the moon lies fair
Upon the straits; – on the French coast the light
Gleams and is gone; the cliffs of England stand,
Glimmering and vast, out in the tranquil bay.
Come to the window, sweet is the night-air!
Only, from the long line of spray
Where the sea meets the moon-blanched land
Listen! you hear the grating roar
Of pebbles which the waves draw back, and fling,
At their return, up the high strand,
Begin, and cease, and then again begin,
With tremulous cadence slow, and bring
The eternal note of sadness in.

Sophocles long ago
Heard it on the Aegaean, and it brought
Into his mind the turbid ebb and flow
Of human misery; we
Find also in the sound a thought,
Hearing it by this distant northern sea.

The Sea of Faith
Was once, too, at the full, and round earth's shore
Lay like the folds of a bright girdle furled;
But now I only hear
Its melancholy, long, withdrawing roar,
Retreating to the breath
Of the night-wind down the vast edges drear
And naked shingles of the world.

Ah, love, let us be true
To one another! for the world, which seems
To lie before us like a land of dreams,
So various, so beautiful, so new,
Hath really neither joy, nor love, nor light,
Nor certitude, nor peace, nor help for pain;

And we are here as on a darkling plain
Swept with confused alarms of struggle and flight,
Where ignorant armies clash by night.

One of my leisure-time pleasures when I'm not planning murder and fabricating clues is exploring churches. Apart from their architectural interest, the commemorative tablets and the carved gravestones give a fascinating insight into the lives and deaths of our forefathers. Very sensibly, today we prefer cremation and we aren't much given to putting up tablets so our descendants will be denied these intimate records of social history.

These words are carved above the west door of Staunton Harold church in Leicestershire.

In the yeare 1653
When all things sacred were throughout ye nation
Either demolisht or profaned
Sir Robert Shirley, Barronet,
Founded this church;
Whose singular praise it is,
to haue done the best things in ye worst times,
and
hoped them in the most callamitous.

The righteous shall be had in everlasting remembrance.

Those were brave words to incise in stone during the Common-wealth; Cromwell, furious, retaliated by saying that anyone who could should provide the money to raise a regiment. Sir Robert, who had never made any secret of his loyalty to the King, refused. He was sent to the Tower and died there, aged twenty-seven.

One of my personal pleasures, and I suspect I share it with many writers, is rummaging around second-hand bookshops and market stalls. To the addict of the written word the mere handling of old books, the potent smell of paper and print, the dusty ambience of these treasure houses is an unfailing delight. And there is always the chance of a find. An out-of-print favourite, a beautifully produced copy of a classic, or an anthol-ogy which can introduce me to new poems and writers I've neglected. And then there are the marvellous oddities, the curious, bizarre or entertaining pieces which provide their moments of pleasure. It was in a long-out-of-print anthology that I discovered the following description of how the well conducted household should start the day.

A Good Wife Begins the Day – from *The Philosophy of Housekeeping*
ISABELLA MARY BEETON

A MISTRESS should rise at latest 7 o'clock. This will appear dreadfully late to some notables, but will be found to be a good hour all the year round. The Mistress should take her cold bath, and perform a neat, careful, and pretty morning toilet. Having performed this careful toilet, she will be ready to descend at 8 o'clock, but before leaving her room will place two chairs at the end of the bed, and turn the whole of the bedclothes over them, and, except on very rainy mornings, will throw open the windows of her room. She should then fold her own and husband's night-dress, which have been airing during her toilet, and place them in their ornamental cover; she will put brushes, combs, hairpins, etc, in their proper places, and leave her toilet-table clear and tidy, and make the whole room as neat as possible. Key-basket in hand, she should descend to the breakfast-room, at once ring for the kettle or tea-urn, according to the season, and make the tea, coffee, cocoa, or chocolate, as the case may be. Her eyes should now glance over the table to see that everything required for the table is in its place, and that all is neatly arranged and ready for the family – flowers on the table, preserve and marmalade in cut-glass dishes . . . When it is possible to get the Master to enjoy an eight o'clock breakfast, household matters go charmingly. He is usually out of the house by nine, and by that hour the windows are wide open, every door set open (weather permitting), and a thorough draught of 'delicious air' is passed through the whole dwelling. AS SOON AS THE MISTRESS hears her husband's step, the bell should be rung for the hot dish; and should he be, as business men usually are, rather pressed for time, she should herself wait on him, cutting his bread, buttering his toast, etc. Also give standing orders that coat, hat, and umbrella shall be brushed and ready; and see that they are, by helping on the coat, handing the hat, and glancing at the umbrella.

In my part of London, setting every door open for a rush of delicious air would invite a rush of undelicious burglars. But at least the wives listening can ensure that their husband's night-dress is in its ornamental cover before feeding him his buttered toast.

My next poem, 'The Toys' by the nineteenth-century poet and critic Coventry Patmore, makes a direct appeal to the reader because the deeply felt emotion it describes is one most of us have known; the tenderness, the pity and the occasional blindness and irritations of parental love. And if the parallel drawn with divine love is obvious, it has seldom been expressed with more sincerity or grace.

The Toys
COVENTRY PATMORE

My little Son, who looked from thoughtful eyes
And moved and spoke in quiet grown-up wise,
Having my law the seventh time disobeyed,
I struck him, and dismissed
With hard words and unkissed,
– His Mother, who was patient, being dead.
Then, fearing lest his grief should hinder sleep,
I visited his bed,
But found him slumbering deep,
With darkened eyelids, and their lashes yet
From his late sobbing wet.
And I, with moan,
Kissing away his tears, left others of my own;
For, on a table drawn beside his head,
He had put, within his reach,
A box of counters and a red-veined stone,
A piece of glass abraded by the beach,
And six or seven shells,
A bottle with bluebells,
And two French copper coins, ranged there with careful art,
To comfort his sad heart.

So when that night I prayed
To God, I wept, and said:
'Ah, when at last we lie with trancèd breath,

Not vexing Thee in death,
And Thou rememberest of what toys
We made our joys,
How weakly understood
Thy great commanded good,
Then, fatherly not less
Than I whom Thou hast moulded from the clay,
Thou'lt leave Thy wrath, and say,
"I will be sorry for their childishness"'.

Readers: Roy Marsden, Sheila Mitchell

Full Selection:
Pride and Prejudice, JANE AUSTEN
Pslam 139
Afterwards, THOMAS HARDY
As I Walked Out One Evening, W. H. AUDEN
Thou Art Indeed Just, Lord, GERARD MANLEY HOPKINS
Dover Beach, MATTHEW ARNOLD
Epitaphs (Bath Abbey and Staunton Harold)
Pot Pourri from a Surrey Garden, JOHN BETJEMAN
The Explosion, PHILIP LARKIN
The Philosophy of Housekeeping, ISABELLA MARY BEETON
The Toys, COVENTRY PATMORE
My Last Duchess, ROBERT BROWNING
The Inquest, W. H. DAVIES
Strychnine in the Soup, P. G. WODEHOUSE
Sonnet CVXI, WILLIAM SHAKESPEARE

DAME CELIA JOHNSON

1982

This programme was recorded shortly before Dame Celia's death. The fact is worth mentioning because on the tape she sounds joyous and full of life. Indeed, when I was asked to choose four programmes particularly worthy of a further repeat during Christmas week 1985, hers was one of the ones that was especially recommended to me. I was happy to include it, both for the pleasure of hearing again not only Dame Celia's voice, but that of David Davis, the much-loved 'Uncle David' from 'Children's Hour', who, along with Rosalind Shanks and Dame Celia herself, was one of the readers. A small mystery was resolved after that broadcast: one item, apparently found 'by the friend of a friend of a friend of a friend in a parish magazine', author unknown, was introduced as 'The Lord Said Unto Noah'. It was enormously popular and dozens of letters arrived from listeners after each transmission asking where it was possible to obtain a copy. After the Christmas broadcast we received a 'phone call from Keith Waterhouse's assistant. It turned out that he had written it for his 'Daily Mirror' column under the title 'How Long, O Lord . . . ?' I am pleased to give due acknowledgement here.

Let me tell you it's not at all easy – one starts to look for a poem, and before you know where you are, you're knee deep in anthologies and collected works and odd scraps of paper to be used as bookmarks. Looking for a poem you find on the way poems you'd forgotten, lots you'd never known, poems you used to like and now like less and, of course, the other way around. It's all very enjoyable, but you decide to decide tomorrow. The poems are bad enough, but prose is impossible. In the end, I almost used a pin. A pin, or a peg to hang things on. My peg to start with is with places that have delighted me.

I'm now going to Greece, to be bewitched by the dolphins and the purple seas and the purple past, mixed with the scent of the wild flowers and herbs, at the almost purple present.

The Old Ships
JAMES ELROY FLECKER

I have seen old ships sail like swans asleep
Beyond the village which men still call Tyre,
With leaden age o'ercargoed, dipping deep
For Famagusta and the hidden sun
That rings black Cyprus with a lake of fire;
And all those ships were certainly so old
Who knows how oft with squat and noisy gun,
Questing brown slaves or Syrian oranges,
The pirates Genoese
Hell-raked them till they rolled
Blood, water, fruit and corpses up the hold.
But now through friendly seas they softly run,
Painted the mid-sea blue or shore-sea green,
Still patterned with the vine and grapes in gold.

But I have seen,
Pointing her shapely shadows from the dawn
And image tumbled on a rose-swept bay,
A drowsy ship of some yet older day;
And, wonder's breath indrawn,
Thought I – who knows – who knows – but in that same
(Fished up beyond Æaea, patched up new
– Stern painted brighter blue –)
That talkative, bald-headed seaman came
(Twelve patient comrades sweating at the oar)
From Troy's doom-crimson shore,
And with great lies about his wooden horse
Set the crew laughing, and forgot his course.

It was so old a ship – who knows – who knows?
– And yet so beautiful, I watched in vain
To see the mast burst open with a rose,
And the whole deck put on its leaves again.

I've always liked poems that tell stories, and the next poem does just that. I read 'The Queen's Marie' once when I was in Hong Kong to some Chinese schoolchildren. They gazed at me with black, beautiful, unwinking eyes, they must have been astounded, but I suppose it was only a proof if proof were needed, of the bewildering idiocy of grown-ups – why should I read them this?

The Queen's Marie

TRAD.

Marie Hamilton's to the kirk gane,
  Wi' ribbons in her hair;
The King thought mair o' Marie Hamilton
  Than ony that were there.

Marie Hamilton's to the kirk gane,
  Wi' ribbons on her breast;
The King thought mair o' Marie Hamilton
  Than he listen'd to the priest.

Marie Hamilton's to the kirk gane
  Wi' gloves upon her hands;
The King thought mair o' Marie Hamilton
  Than the Queen and a' her lands.

She hadna been about the King's court
  A month, but barely ane,
Till she was beloved by a' the King's court,
  And the King the only man.

She hadna been about the King's court
  A month, but barely three,
Till frae the King's court Marie Hamilton,
  Marie Hamilton durstna be.

The King is to the Abbey gane,
  To pu' the Abbey tree,
To scale the babe frae Marie's heart;
  But the thing it wadna be.

O she has row'd it in her apron,
  And set it on the sea –

'Gae sink ye or swim ye, bonny babe,
  Ye'se get nae mair o' me.'

Word is to the kitchen gane,
  And word is to the ha',
And word is to the noble room
  Amang the ladies a',
That Marie Hamilton's brought to bed,
  And the bonny babe's miss'd and awa'.

Scarcely had she lain down again,
  And scarcely fa'en asleep,
When up and started our gude Queen
  Just at her bed-feet;
Saying – Marie Hamilton, where's your babe?
  For I am sure I heard it greet.

'O no, O no, my noble Queen!
  Think no sic thing to be;
'Twas but a stitch into my side,
  And sair it troubles me!'

'Get up, get up, Marie Hamilton:
  Get up and follow me;
For I am going to Edinburgh town,
  A rich wedding for to see.'

O slowly, slowly rase she up,
  And slowly put she on;
And slowly rade she out the way
  Wi' mony a weary groan.

The Queen was clad in scarlet,
  Her merry maids all in green;
And every town that they cam to,
  They took Marie for the Queen.

'Ride hooly, hooly, gentlemen,
  Ride hooly now wi' me!
For never, I am sure, a wearier burd
  Rade in your companie.'

But little wist Marie Hamilton,
   When she rade on the brown,
That she was gaen to Edinburgh town,
   And a' to be put down.

'Why weep ye sae, ye burgess wives,
   Why look ye sae on me?
O I am going to Edinburgh town,
   A rich wedding to see.'

When she gaed up the tolbooth stairs,
   The corks frae her heels did flee;
And lang or e'er she cam down again,
   She was condemmed to die.

When she cam to the Netherbow port,
   She laugh'd loud laughters three;
But when she cam to the gallows foot
   The tears blinded her e'e.

'Yestreen the Queen had four Maries,
   The night she'll hae but three;
There was Marie Seaton, and Marie Beaton,
   And Marie Carmichael, and me.

No one really seems to know who wrote this next piece. Rumour has it that it was found by a friend of a friend of a friend of a friend in a parish magazine. But perhaps somebody may claim it.

How Long, O Lord . . . ?
KEITH WATERHOUSE

And God said unto Noah, Make thee an ark of gopher wood; rooms shalt thou make in the ark, and the length of the ark shall be 300 cubits.

And of every living thing of all flesh, two of every sort shalt thou bring into the ark, to keep them alive with thee.

And Noah said, Sign here, and leavest Thou a deposit.

And the Lord signed there, and left He a deposit.

And Noah was 600 years old when the flood of waters was upon the Earth.

And the Lord said unto Noah, Where is the ark, which I commanded thee to build?

An Noah said unto the Lord, Verily, I have had three carpenters off ill.

The gopher wood supplier hath let me down – yea even though the gopher wood hath been on order for nigh upon 12 months. The damp-course specialist hath not turned up. What can I do, O Lord?

And God said unto Noah, I want that ark finished even after seven days and seven nights.

And Noah said, It will be so.

And it was not so.

And the Lord said unto Noah, What seemeth to be the trouble this time?

And Noah said unto the Lord, Mine sub-contractor hath gone bankrupt. The pitch which Thou commandest me to put on the outside and on the inside of the ark hath not arrived. The plumber hath gone on strike.

Noah rent his garments and said, The glazier departeth on holiday to Majorca – yea, even though I offerest him double time. Shem, my son, who helpeth me on the ark side of the business, hath formed a pop group with his brothers Ham and Japheth. Lord I am undone.

And God said in his wrath, Noah, do not thou mucketh Me about.

The end of all flesh is come before me for the Earth is filled with violence through them; and behold, I will destroy them with the Earth. How can I destroy them with the Earth if thou art incapable of completing the job that thou was contracted to do?

And Noah said, Lo, the contract will be fulfilled.

And Lo, it was not fulfilled.

And Noah said unto the Lord, The gopher wood is definitely in the warehouse. Verily, and the gopher wood supplier waiteth only upon his servant to find the invoices before he delivereth the gopher wood unto me.

And the Lord grew angry and said, Scrubbeth thou round the gopher wood. What about the animals?

Of fowls after their kind, and of cattle after their kind, of every creeping thing of the Earth after his kind, two of every sort have I ordered to come unto thee, to keep them alive.

Where for example are the giraffes?

And Noah said unto the Lord, They are expected today.

And the Lord said unto Noah, And where are the clean beasts, the male and the female; to keep their seed alive upon the face of all the Earth?

And Noah said, The van cometh on Tuesday; yea and yea, it will be so.

And the Lord said unto Noah, How about the unicorns?

And Noah wrung his hands and wept, saying, Lord, Lord, they are a discontinued line. Thou canst not get unicorns for love nor money.

And God said, Come thou, Noah, I have left with thee a deposit, and thou hast signed a contract.

Where are the monkeys, and the bears, and the hippopotami, and the elephants, and the zebras and the hartebeests, two of each kind, and of fowls also of the air by sevens, the male and the female?

And Noah said unto the Lord, They have been delivered unto the wrong address, but should arrive on Friday; all save the fowls of the air by sevens, for it hath just been told unto me that fowls of the air are sold only in half-dozens.

And God said unto Noah, Thou hast not made an ark of gopher wood, nor hast thou lined it with pitch within and without; and of every living thing of all flesh, two of every sort hast thou failed to bring into the ark. What sayest thou, Noah?

And Noah kissed the Earth and said, Lord, thou knowest in thy wisdom what it is like with delivery dates.

And the Lord in his wisdom said, Noah, my son, I knowest. Why else dost thou think I have caused a flood to descend upon the Earth?

Readers: David Davis, Rosalind Shanks

Full Selection:
A Smuggler's Song, RUDYARD KIPLING
Tregardock, JOHN BETJEMAN

THE EARL OF LICHFIELD

1982

The last item in this programme is another one that gave rise to a rush of letters from listeners. It seems not to have been published widely, so I am pleased to include it here. The impression of Lord Lichfield that comes across from his script is very different from that given by the barbed ramblings of the popular press. He is clearly a sensitive man with a deep feeling for and love of things English. These include the game of cricket, a blind spot of mine, and English humour. Recovering from appendicitis, when he was 15, he read 'The Cricket Match' and 'England Their England' by A. G. MacDonell. His mother had given him the book to cheer him up. He laughed so much while reading it that his stitches burst.

An ancient and distant relation of mine once laid out a cricket pitch, and being rather a grand Duke he felt that it was only right and proper that the grandest cricketer in the land should come to open it for him, and so he chose Dr Grace. And there was a blacksmith, who on arriving at the crease bowled a perfectly accurate ball which struck the gallant and noble doctor on the knee but plumb. A great shout of 'How's that?' went up. Before the umpire could get his hands out of his pocket, Dr Grace walked down the wicket and said 'Young man, these thousand people have come to watch me bat, not you bowl.'

When I was asked by the producer of this programme, Brian Patten, to think about what I would like to include in the programme, I was lecturing on the QE2 just before she was requisitioned to go to the Falklands and I spent a few hours in the library there just before she went. I have chosen a number of things which come very much from my childhood and I make no apology for being patriotic and rather 'Boys' Own' about the whole thing.

This piece is a personal one and rather obscure. In 1740 Admiral Anson, who happened to be a great-great-great-great-great-great-great-uncle of mine, left Staffordshire and set off around the world to harass the Spaniards and to come back with any treasure to be found on an incredibly enriched galleon which sailed between Acapulco and Manila. He left England with eight ships in 1740 and finally arrived back in 1744. But on April 13th 1741, which I imagine must have been a Friday, there was recorded a piece about his attempting to round Cape Horn.

Log of The Centurion
LEO HEAPS

Edward Legge of the Severn and George Murray of the Pearle turned back after several unsuccessful attempts to round the Cape and ran off before the gales to the River Plate, eventually reaching Rio de Janeiro.

Their crews were no more disabled than the crews of the other ships, and they would have been no worse off had they remained with the squadron. The presence of two more fighting ships in the Pacific might have changed the course of history for Britain. Anson at the time presumed the Severn and Pearle had been lost.

Their commanders' reasons for returning were irrefutable. It seemed that they simply could not go on. They had reached the end. In fact there was no plausible reason for anyone continuing beyond the Horn in the face of more certain destruction. Except that brave men differed. Under the ultimate test Anson had a will that could not be weakened by adversity. So had Saumarez. Those fine, slight differences in human nature, never quite apparent until the final crisis, now showed themselves among the men. Colonel Cracherode, colonel of a dying force of marines, also clung grimly to life. He was a battered veteran of a dozen wars and survived to lead his pitiful remnants against the Spaniards at Payta in Chile. After Anson himself, the character of Philip Saumarez dominated. Perhaps the quiet, tortured nature of the man had been inhibited too long in the rigid cast of the Navy, and at last Anson gave Saumarez the chance he wanted. In many ways the rounding of Cape Horn in the Tryall was the making of Saumarez.

For over a month the squadron attempted to gain the west coast of Patagonia and leave behind the bleak, wild isthmus of Tierra del Fuego. The isthmus projected like a curved beak on the extremity of South America, bent back by untold centuries of severe storms.

In the conflicting streams and winds the ships were flung about like small boats. One man on the Centurion broke a collar bone, several fractured their legs and arms, while two seamen were thrown overboard and lost. From March to May there were almost continuous storms on an unprecedented scale.

Water constantly flooded the decks of all the ships, especially the Tryall, straining ahead of the squadron with the seas cascading like waterfalls from the plunging bows. Towards the middle of April, 'there came a storm which both in its violence and continuation exceeded all that hitherto encountered'. It lasted three days. On the last day the quarter gallery of the Centurion near the poop was stoved in and water 'rushed into the ship like a deluge'. Shrouds broke and for days the Centurion lay under the bare poles, heaving and crashing helplessly into the seas until the storm gradually subsided.

Almost everyone was infected with the scurvy and badly demoralised. Forty men had been lost since they came through the Le Maire Straits and most of the crew unable to perform their duties. On each watch no more than seventy seamen could be mustered, while the marines were all either sick or dead.

What's extraordinary about that is that it was 241 years ago and yet we still had to sail down to the South Seas not so long ago in much the same way. He went on with that beleaguered ship. In fact out of 1,939 men only 101 arrived back in England. After putting out the Great Fire of Canton on their way back, he arrived home and produced 39 wagons of silver which were taken to the tower of London and then distributed according to rank and the residue that he had went to build the house that I live in, which is called Shugborough. But it does demonstrate that the kind of spirit that existed then is something that I'm afraid keeps going through my choices, but I make no apology for that.

I want to go on to something quite different. I've always thought that if people become famous too early they're likely to reach a sticky end – in fact it always worries me that perhaps I've had a bit too much publicity myself, and what will it be like next year? And hence I go on to Oscar Wilde, not the Wilde you might expect, not the prose, but 'The Ballad of Reading Gaol' which, of course, is late in Wilde's literary career, and somehow there's something very touching in this. The sentiment is that of 'Well, I'm pretty badly off, but there's always somebody worse around the corner.'

The Ballad of Reading Gaol
OSCAR WILDE

He did not wear his scarlet coat,
    For blood and wine are red,
And blood and wine were on his hands
    When they found him with the dead,
The poor dead woman whom he loved,
    And murdered in her bed.

He walked amongst the Trial Men
    In a suit of shabby grey;
A cricket cap was on his head,

And his step seemed light and gay;
But I never saw a man who looked
  So wistfully at the day.

I never saw a man who looked
  With such a wistful eye
Upon that little tent of blue
  Which prisoners call the sky,
And at every drifting cloud that went
  With sails of silver by.

I walked, with other souls in pain,
  Within another ring,
And was wondering if the man had done
  A great or little thing,
When a voice behind me whispered low,
  'That fellow's got to swing.'

Dear Christ! the very prison walls
  Suddenly seemed to reel,
And the sky above my head became
  Like a casque of scorching steel;
And, though I was a soul in pain,
  My pain I could not feel.

I only knew what hunted thought
  Quickened his step, and why
He looked upon the garish day
  With such a wistful eye;
The man had killed the thing he loved,
  And so he had to die.

Yet each man kills the thing he loves,
  By each let this be heard,
Some do it with a bitter look,
  Some with a flattering word.
The coward does it with a kiss,
  The brave man with a sword!

Some kill their love when they are young,
  And some when they are old;
Some strangle with the hands of Lust,

Some with the hands of Gold:
The kindest use a knife, because
The dead so soon grow cold.

Some love too little, some too long,
Some sell, and others buy;
Some do the deed with many tears,
And some without a sigh;
For each man kills the thing he loves,
Yet each man does not die.

This last piece was shown to me after the death of an exceedingly dear relation and I was asked to read it in an exceedingly beautiful church. It quite simply had one effect on me in that it provided me with a completely new feeling that I hadn't thought I would experience after somebody had died. It's by Henry Scott Holland.

Death is nothing at all, . . . I have only slipped away into the next room . . . I am I and you are you . . . whatever we were to each other that we are still. Call me by my old familiar name, speak to me in the easy way which you always used. Put no difference into your tone; wear no forced air of solemnity or sorrow. Laugh as we always laughed at the little jokes we enjoyed together. Play, smile, think of me, pray for me. Let my name be ever the household word it always was. Let it be spoken without effect, without the ghost of a shadow on it. Life means all that it ever meant. It is the same as it ever was; there is an absolutely unbroken continuity. What is this death but a negligible accident? Why should I be out of mind because I am out of sight? I am but waiting for you, for an interval, somewhere very near just around the corner . . . All is well.

Readers: Robert Hardy, Frank Windsor

Full Selection:
Lord Lundy, HILAIRE BELLOC
Summoned by Bells, JOHN BETJEMAN
England, Their England, A. G. MACDONELL

Log of The Centurion, LEO HEAPS
The Ballad of Reading Gaol, OSCAR WILDE
Preface to the Doctor's Dilemma, BERNARD SHAW
The Second World War, Volume 2, SIR WINSTON CHURCHILL
Speech to Schoolchildren of Rotorua, 3 March 1958, LORD COBHAM
Forty Years On, ALAN BENNETT
Death is Nothing at All . . . , HENRY SCOTT HOLLAND

PROFESSOR SIR BERNARD LOVELL

1978

The learned astronomer from Jodrell Bank is clearly in love with the firmament and like all good scientists has the soul of a poet. He calculated that every year nearly a ton of books, papers and letters thud on to his desk and that these comprised most of his prose reading. Whilst paying them due professional attention, he was clearly not impressed with the quality of language in which the findings were expressed. As an example of what he so disliked he quoted a typical present-day description of the awe-inspiring sight of the launch of a huge balloon full of scientific apparatus and its ascent to a great height which began: 'The balloon was launched at 1204 UT and reached a float altitude of $2.9g\ cm^{-2}$ at approximately 1530 UT where it remained for 6.5h before cutdown.' – and a recent account of the evolution of the Universe: 'it is generally believed that in the physically realistic case, an incomplete causal geodisc terminates in a singularity which destroys everything which enters . . .' – including sense and meaning presumably. He compared such modern scientific expression unfavourably with that of the great scientists of the past. Who can blame him?

167

Nowadays I suppose that a quarter of a century is a long time to work in the same place, but I've worked here at Jodrell Bank for even longer than that – since the end of the war in fact. First in ex-army trailers amongst the corn fields, then amongst the mud and cranes as the steelwork of the great telescope rose above the Cheshire plain. Twenty years ago the massive bowl of the telescope began to probe the sky as it is doing tonight, searching far into time and space for answers to the problems of the universe. It's an exciting and romantic place, especially at night when the telephones no longer ring, and the huge structure stands isolated in the floodlights against the dark of the sky, as it is outside on this dome now.

This Planetarium is very close to that telescope. Many thousands of people visit here every year to see the stars and planets projected on to the dome. Now it is full of my friends and colleagues; I hope I am not going to bore you like Walt Whitman's 'The Learned Astronomer'.

When I Heard the Learn'd Astronomer
WALT WHITMAN

When I heard the learn'd astronomer,
When the proofs, the figures, were ranged
    in columns before me,
When I was shown the charts and diagrams, to add,
    divide, and measure them,
When I sitting heard the astronomer where he lectured
    with much applause in the lecture room,
How soon unnaccountable I became tired and sick,
Till rising and gliding out I wandere'd off by myself,
In the mystical moist night-air, and from time to time,
Look'd up in perfect silence at the stars.

I can't help contrasting modern scientific prose with that I read as a young student. Two years ago the Council of the Royal Society allocated to me the task of writing the biographical memoir of Lord Blackett. For over 40 years he had been a major influence in my life and work and naturally I wanted to do this job thoroughly. So I collected and read more than 130 scientific papers, books and other articles which he had written. His prose was always good and often magnificent. As a young man he was a lieutenant in the Royal Navy and his diaries contain a graphic account of the Battle of Jutland. In 1919 he decided to leave the Navy and joined Rutherford's team in the Cavendish Laboratory. Within a few years he had obtained results in nuclear physics of such importance that they are described in every textbook of physics.

I wish the young scientists today would read those original papers, written between 1920 and 1930 – the elegance and simplicity of the style in which he describes his work is memorable. Here is a part of his description of the apparatus which he used to study the disintegration of the nitrogen atom by alpha-particles. He is describing the problem of achieving a vacuum in his apparatus:

So usually an apparatus of this type is made in sections, these being fitted together and made tight against a leakage of air into the apparatus by the use of a grease or cement. It is curious that the most universally successful vacuum cement available for many years should have been a material of common use for quite other purposes. At one time it might have been hard to find in an English laboratory an apparatus which did not use red Bank of England sealing-wax as a vacuum cement. If its pre-eminence is now being shaken, it is not by some refined product of laborious research but by ordinary plasticine. It is hardly possible to exaggerate the controlling importance of such simple technical matters, however trivial they may seem to be.

We've been part of the technical revolution of the age: the telescope records signals which had their origin in remote space billions of years ago and started on their journey to us long before our own Earth came into existence. Even so, we often feel as Milton did 300 years ago. In Book 7 of 'Paradise Lost', Raphael explained to Adam how the World was first created. At the beginning of Book 8, Adam makes further enquiries concerning the celestial motions.

Paradise Lost Book 8
JOHN MILTON

When I behold this goodly Frame, this World
Of Heav'n and Earth consisting, and compute
Thir magnitudes, this Earth a spot, a graine,
An Atom, with the Firmanent compar'd
And all her numberd Starrs, that seem to rowle
Spaces incomprehensible (for such
Thir distance argues and thir swift return
Diurnal) meerly to officiate light
Round this opacous Earth, this punctual spot,
One day and night; in all thir vast survey
Useless besides, reasoning I oft admire,
How Nature wise and frugal could commit
Such disproportions, with superfluous hand
So many nobler Bodies to create.

In 1638, twenty-nine years before the publication of 'Paradise Lost', Milton had travelled to Italy. The country was still distracted by the trial and imprisonment of Galileo. In the Areopagitica – the address which Milton made to Parliament pleading for the freedom of the Press – he wrote:

Areopagitica
JOHN MILTON

I have sat among their learned men and been counted happy to be born in such a place of philosophic freedom as they supposed England was, while they themselves did nothing but bemoan the servile conditions into which learning amongst them was brought; that this was it which had damped the glory of Italian wits, that nothing had been there written now these many years but flattery and fustian. There it was that I found and visited the famous Galileo, grown old, a prisoner of the Inquisition.

The intellectual stability of the Western World had been based on the belief that the Earth was fixed in space at the centre of the Universe. In order to explain the varying positions of the planets in the sky a complex system of motions of the heavenly bodies around the Earth in epicycles had been devised. Galileo's crime was that he was the first to look at the heavens through a small telescope and so to find the observational evidence that the earth was not fixed in space, but was in motion around the Sun.

A generation later Milton placed the argument about the movement of the Earth, and about the geometrical description of the motions of the heavenly bodies in epicycles, in the ethereal context of Plato's moving image of eternity. In this marvellous passage Raphael is continuing his explanation to Adam.

Paradise Lost Book 8
JOHN MILTON

Hereafter, when they come to model Heav'n
And calculate the Starrs, how they will weild
The mightie frame, how build, unbuild, contrive
To save appeerances, how gird the Sphear
With Centric and Eccentric scribl'd o're,
Cycle and Epicycle, Orb in Orb:
Alreadie by thy reasoning this I guess,
Who art to lead thy ofspring, and supposest
That Bodies bright and greater should not serve
The less not bright, nor Heav'n such journies run,
Earth sitting still, when she alone receaves
The benefit: consider first, that Great
Or Bright inferrs not Excellence: the Earth
Though, in comparison of Heav'n, so small,
Nor glistering, may of solid good containe
More plenty then the Sun that barren shines,
Whose vertue on it self works no effect,
But in the fruitful Earth; there first receavd
His beams, unactive else, thir vigor find.
Yet not to Earth are those bright Luminaries
Officious, but to thee Earths habitant
And for the Heav'ns wide Circuit, let it speak
The Makers high magnificence, who built
So spacious, and his Line stretcht out so farr;
That Man may know he dwells not in his own;
An Edifice too large for him to fill
Lodg'd in a small partition, and the rest
Ordain'd for uses to his Lord best known.

The swiftness of those Circles attribute,
Though numberless, to his Omnipotence,
That to corporeal substances could adde
Speed almost Spiritual; mee thou thinkst not slow,
Who since the Morning hour set out from Heav'n
Where God resides, and ere mid-day arriv'd
In *Eden*, distance inexpressible
By numbers that have name. But this I urge,
Admitting Motion in the Heav'ns, to shew
Invalid that which thee to doubt it mov'd;
Not that I so affirm, though so it seem
To thee who hast thy dwelling here on Earth.
God to remove his wayes from human sense,
Plac'd Heav'n from Earth so farr, that earthly sight,
If it presume, might erre in things too high,
And no advantage gaine. What if the Sun
Be Center to the World, and other Starrs
By his attractive vertue and thir own
Incited, dance about him various rounds?
Thir wandring course now high, now low, then hid,
Progressive, retrograde, or standing still,
In six thou seest, and what if sev'nth to these
The Planet Earth, so steadfast though she seem,
Insensibly three different Motions move?

When I was a student I played so much cricket and practised the organ for such long periods that I nearly let down my teachers of science who thought I might have promise.

Since I was a member of three cricket teams – the University, my local village and the Bristol Optimists, this was quite a serious diversion and I suppose I must have played on nearly every cricket ground in Gloucestershire and Somerset. When I finally left the West Country for Manchester I was inconsolably nostalgic and so understood very well the essence of Francis Thompson's poem about Hornby and Barlow. He suffered the same experience – but in reverse. Francis Thompson wrote this poem about a cricket match played at Old Trafford 100 years ago when he was 19 years old – in July 1878, the first time that Lancashire had met Gloucestershire and the fame of W. G. Grace and his brothers

E. M. and G. F. was such that on the last day of that match it's recorded that 16,000 people crammed into Old Trafford and that at least 2,000 of them forced the gates without payment when the ground had been declared full. In Lancashire's second innings Hornby scored a century and Barlow 80.

All of this unexpectedly came to life for me one day last summer. The scene was at a lovely country house in the west of England; outside the dining room windows stretched a perfect small cricket ground. Suddenly I realised that I was enjoying a luncheon with a near relative of the famous Hornby of the Francis Thompson poem!

Incidentally, Francis Thompson was an unsuccessful medical student in the University of Manchester and lived in great poverty until his first book of poems was published (including 'The Hound of Heaven') five years after the events referred to in the poem which we are to hear now. After his failures in Manchester he moved to London in 1907. His nostalgia for Old Trafford was so great that when, late in his life, he was invited to Lord's to watch Middlesex play Lancashire he could not face the ordeal and produced instead this memorable lament.

At Lords
FRANCIS THOMPSON

It is little I repair to the matches of the Southron folk,
    Though my own red roses there may blow;
It is little I repair to the matches of the Southron folk,
    Though the red roses crest the caps, I know.
For the field is full of shades as I near the shadowy coast,
And a ghostly batsman plays to the bowling of a ghost,
And I look through my tears on a soundless-clapping host,
    As the run-stealers flicker to and fro,
      To and fro: –
O my Hornby and my Barlow long ago!

It is Glo'ster coming North, the irresistible,
    The Shire of the Graces, long ago!
It is Gloucestershire up North, the irresistible,
    And new-risen Lancashire the foe!

A Shire so young that has scarce impressed its traces,
Ah, how shall it stand before all resistless Graces?
O, little red rose, their bats are as maces
　　To beat thee down, this summer long ago!

This day of seventy-eight they are come up North against
　　thee,
　　This day of seventy-eight, long ago!
The champion of the centuries, he cometh up against thee,
　　With his brethren, every one a famous foe!
The long-whiskered Doctor, that laugheth rules to scorn,
While the bowler, pitched against him, bans the day that he
　　was born;
And G. F. with his science makes the fairest length forlorn;
　　They are come from the West to work thee woe!

It is little I repair to the matches of the Southron folk,
　　Though my own red roses there may blow;
It is little I repair to the matches of the Southron folk,
　　Though the red roses crest the caps, I know.
For the field is full of shades as I near the shadowy coast,
And a ghostly batsman plays to the bowling of a ghost,
And I look through my tears on a soundless-clapping host,
　　As the run-stealers flicker to and fro,
　　To and fro: –
O my Hornby and my Barlow long ago!

Readers: Patience Collier, Patrick Troughton

Full Selection:
When I heard the Learn'd Astronomer, WALT WHITMAN
Paradise Lost, Book 8, JOHN MILTON
Areopagitica, JOHN MILTON
The Garden, VITA SACKVILLE-WEST
The Land (Summer), VITA SACKVILLE-WEST
The Land (Spring), VITA SACKVILLE-WEST
At Lords, FRANCIS THOMPSON
The Hill, H.A. VACHELL
Autobiography, NEVILLE CARDUS

KIT McMAHON

1985

Normally people who are asked to present 'With Great Pleasure' are at least fairly well-known to the public at large. It's far from being an invariable rule as it is always stimulating to meet and to present to the general listener someone gifted and/or eminent in their field, who is not frequently to be seen or heard on the 'media'. I must admit, however, that when I was approached by Kit McMahon's assistant it was the first time I had seriously considered including a banker in the series, although the Deputy Governor of the Bank of England, as he was then, was obviously not without interest. On meeting him for the first time in his palatial office, I was struck by how far he had already thought the programme through and how quietly enthusiastic he was about the possibility of taking part. He did not strike me as being particularly extrovert, but it was an attractive personality none the less. He turned up at the recording a jolly, friendly and not totally organised man (he had forgotten his notes which comprised the script) whom it was easy to like.

I read an awful lot as a child and adolescent, all kinds of books from rubbish to difficult classics, which I liked less than I pretended. Apart from comics and thrillers, the taste for which has stayed with me for the rest of my life, if I do look back at my later school days and try to think of passages which especially excited me I think I might come up with the following:

If a body is at rest or in a state of uniform motion it will remain so unless acted on by an external force.

or:

To every action there is an equal and opposite reaction.

Newton's first and third laws. The second I have to say is a little bit too complicated to read here.

I can still remember the excitement of being shown this great jump in thought that those laws represented. The wonderful realisation that you needed force not to make something move, but to accelerate it. And ever since I've found scientific laws fascinating for the way in which a statement, which is in some sense just a tautology, can illuminate the real world and stimulate great discovery and achievement. And I may say in passing that against this standard I find the so called laws of economics pretty poor things.

In due course, however, I came to like poetry. I'd like to show you a poem which explores migration. I include it not just because I like it and think it a moving poem, but as an act of piety. Its author, A. D. Hope, Alec Hope, taught me English Literature at Melbourne University; he was the first true, uncompromising artist I'd met and that is always an experience to be grateful for. He is, I think, a very distinguished poet, I believe one of the best to have written in this century, but, at least in England, he is very under-rated – under-rated because under-read. Most anthologists, having to limit their field somewhere, draw the line at the British Isles. You might find a Hope poem in an anthology of Commonwealth verse, but what a ghastly, nonsensical concept to be embedded in. Anyway, I hope that some people will like 'The Death of the Bird' enough to seek out his collected works.

The Death of the Bird
A.D. HOPE

For every bird there is this last migration:
Once more the cooling year kindles her heart;
With a warm passage to the summer station
Love pricks the course in lights across the chart.

Year after year a speck on the map, divided
By a whole hemisphere, summons her to come;
Season after season, sure and safely guided,
Going away she is also coming home.

And being home, memory becomes a passion
With which she feeds her brood and straws her nest,
Aware of ghosts that haunt the heart's possession
And exiled love mourning within the breast.

The sands are green with a mirage of valleys;
The palm tree casts a shadow not its own;
Down the long architrave of temple or palace
Blows a cool air from moorland scraps of stone.

And day by day the whisper of love grows stronger;
That delicate voice, more urgent with despair,
Custom and fear constraining her no longer,
Drives her at last on the waste leagues of air.

A vanishing speck in those inane dominions,
Single and frail, uncertain of her place,
Alone in the bright host of her companions,
Lost in the blue unfriendliness of space.

She feels it close now, the appointed season:
The invisible thread is broken as she flies;
Suddenly, without warning, without reason,
The guiding spark of instinct winks and dies.

Try as she will, the trackless world delivers
No way, the wilderness of light no sign,
The immense and complex map of hills and rivers
Mocks her small wisdom with its vast design.

And darkness rises from the eastern valleys,
And the winds buffer her with their hungry breath,
And the great earth, with neither grief nor malice,
Receives the tiny burden of her death.

I came to England in 1951 and have spent the rest of my life here absorbed in the worlds of economics, finance and public affairs. Enjoyable though that's been, I have to say that searching back through it, it hasn't yielded me passages that I could remember with particular pleasure, at least that could be read out. For my selections, therefore, I shall be drawing on my private life and I would like now to move to three poems on the deepest and most private of emotions, love. I suppose there are more poems on love than on anything else, certainly more bad poems, but perhaps more good ones as well. It took me a long time to select the ones I would most like you to hear. Some I rejected because I think they are too well known, some because, though clearly great poetry, they didn't speak to me or my wife, so I turned for my first selection to the greatest love poet, indeed for me the greatest poet, Yeats. Here is one of his less known poems, certainly not his greatest, but one which seems to me to capture very simply something of the mysterious crash of falling in love.

Her Triumph
W. B. YEATS

I did the dragon's will until you came
Because I had fancied love a casual
Improvisation, or a settled game
That followed if I let the kerchief fall:
Those deeds were best that gave the minute wings
And heavenly music if they gave it wit;
And then you stood among the dragon-wings.
I mocked, being crazy, but you mastered it
And broke the train and set my ankles free,
Saint George or else a pagan Perseus;
And now we stare astonished at the sea,
And a miraculous strange bird shrieks at us.

Next something quite different, about love gone hopelessly wrong. This poem I think is remarkable for its drama and for the amazing way that though it is narrated by one of the two people concerned, it is completely even-handed and objective in its pity for both of them. It is by poor, unhappy Charlotte Mew.

The Farmer's Bride
CHARLOTTE MEW

Three Summers since I chose a maid,
Too young maybe – but more's to do
At harvest-time than bide and woo.
    When us was wed she turned afraid
Of love and me and all things human;
Like the shut of a winter's day.
Her smile went out, and twasn't a woman –
    More like a little frightened fay.
    One night, in the Fall, she runned away.

'Out 'mong the sheep, her be,' they said,
'Should properly have been abed;'
But sure enough she wasn't there
Lying awake with her wide brown stare.
So over seven-acre field and up-along across the down
We chased her, flying like a hare
Before our lanterns. To Church-Town
    All in a shiver and a scare
We caught her, fetched her home at last
    And turned the key upon her, fast.

She does the work about the house
As well as most, but like a mouse:
    Happy enough to chat and play
    With birds and rabbits and such as they,
    So long as men-folk keep away.
'Not near, not near!' her eyes beseech
When one of us comes within reach.
    The women say that beasts in stall
    Look round like children at her call.
    I've hardly heard her speak at all.

179

Shy as a leveret, swift as he,
Straight and slight as a young larch tree,
Sweet as the first wild violets, she,
To her wild self. But what to me?

The short days shorten and the oaks are brown,
    The blue smoke rises to the low grey sky,
One leaf in the still air falls slowly down,
    A magpie's spotted feathers lie
On the black earth spread white with rime,
The berries redden up to Christmas-time.
    What's Christmas-time without there be
    Some other in the house than we!

She sleeps up in the attic there
Alone, poor maid. 'Tis but a stair
Betwixt us. Oh! my God! the down,
    The soft young down of her, the brown,
The brown of her – her eyes, her hair, her hair!

A third love poem has given a great deal of pleasure to my wife and myself. It celebrates a very good emotion indeed, an emotion perhaps under some threat as the sexual revolution going on around us marches inexorably forward, the straightforward emotion of sexual affection. It is by Sir John Harington who lived from 1560–1612 and is best known for a major work which I confess never to have opened. But he also wrote a number of *jeux d'esprit* and this is one of them.

The Author to His Wife, of a Woman's Eloquence
JOHN HARRINGTON

My Mall, I mark that when you mean to prove me
To buy a velvet gown, or some rich border,
Thou callst me good sweet heart, thou swearst to
      love me,
Thy locks, thy lips, thy looks, speak all in order,
Thou thinks't, and right thou thinks't, that these
      do move me,
That all these severally thy suit do further:

> But shall I tell thee what most thy suit
>   advances?
> Thy fair smoothe words? no, no, thy fair
>   smoothe haunches.

In the last few years Norfolk has become an important part of my
life, we spend most weekends and many holidays there, and I've
chosen, therefore, two Norfolk pieces. The first is a little poem by
Frances Cornford, the author, you may remember, of that splendid poem that begins: 'Oh fat white woman whom nobody loves,
why do you walk through the fields in gloves, missing so much
and so much?' This poem is called 'The Coast: Norfolk' and was
written, I suppose, 70 or 80 years ago, but it seems to us still to
catch the space and feel of that lovely, remote, windswept
county.

The Coast: Norfolk
FRANCES CORNFORD

As on the highway's quiet edge
He mows the grass beside the hedge,
The old man has for company
The distant, grey, salt-smelling sea,
A poppied field, a cow, and calf,
The finches on the telegraph.

Across his faded back a hoe,
He slowly, slowly scythes alone
In silence of the wind-soft air,
With ladies' bedstraw everywhere,
With whitened corn, and tarry poles,
And far-off gulls like risen souls.

My second piece on Norfolk is rather a swizz. It's a passage from
Thomas Browne, 'Urne Burial'. I managed to include it under
Norfolk because Sir Thomas Browne was a seventeenth-century
doctor in Norwich with a wide-ranging curiosity and a mind well
stocked with classical scholarship. He attracts me as a kind of
mid-point between old scholasticism and the beginning of modern science with the Royal Society. In his very minor way he

seems to exemplify Britain's greatest century, the seventeenth. He loved to investigate in an apparently scientific way problems scarcely amenable to that approach. For example, one of his essays devotes a good deal of time to trying, in the end unsuccessfully, to establish exactly what fruit it was that Eve gave Adam. This extract, a famous one, concerns some ancient burial urns which a friend of his had found dug up in Walsingham, which is very near us in Norfolk. Sir Thomas Browne muses a good deal on the urns themselves, who buried them there and why, and expresses the magnitude of his problem in the following words:

Urne Burial
SIR THOMAS BROWNE

What song the Syrens sang, or what name Achilles assumed when he hid himself among women, though puzzling questions are not beyond all conjecture. What time the persons of these Ossuaries entered the famous Nations of the dead, and slept with Princes and Counsellors, might admit a wide solution. But who were the proprietaries of these bones, or what bodies these ashes made up, were a question above Antiquarism. Not to be resolved by man, nor easily perhaps by spirits, except we consult the Provincial Guardians, or tutelary Observators. Had they made as good provision for their names, as they have done for their Reliques, they had not so grossly erred in the art of perpetuation. But to subsist in bones, and be but Pyramidally extant, is a fallacy in duration. Vain ashes, which in the oblivion of names, person, times, and sexes, have found unto themselves a fruitlesse continuation, and only arise unto late posterity, as Emblemes of mortal vanities; Antidotes against pride, vainglory, and madding vices.

Readers: Dinsdale Landen, Jane Lapotaire

Full Selection:
Treasure Island, R. L. STEVENSON
The Windhover, GERARD MANLEY HOPKINS
The Death of the Bird, A. D. HOPE

The Big Sleep, RAYMOND CHANDLER
Her Triumph, W. B. YEATS
The Farmer's Bride, CHARLOTTE MEW
My Mall, JOHN HARRINGTON
Ulysses, JAMES JOYCE
The Coast: Norfolk, FRANCES CORNFORD
Urne-Burial, SIR THOMAS BROWNE
Musée des Beaux Arts, W. H. AUDEN
Life with Picasso, FRANCOISE GELOT
A Song to David, CHRISTOPHER SMART

JOHN MORTIMER

1978

John Mortimer is the only person who has deliberately been commissioned twice to take part in 'With Great Pleasure'. One other person, also a famous writer, had been, but it was an accident. On that occasion, neither the producer, nor the writer, remembered that he had done one before! In Mortimer's case, however, the second programme was not in his own name, but was written around a non-existent American author as an April Fool joke. I do remember, however, about twenty years ago working as a 'spot' operator – opening and shutting doors, pouring tea and generally clattering around – on the re-make of Mortimer's radio play 'A Voyage Around My Father', the original tapes having been mislaid or wiped. Three or four years later when I was, briefly, an assistant producer in Television Centre, the BBC announced with a great fanfare a season of new plays by major playwrights specially written for television. One of them was called 'A Voyage Around My father' by John Mortimer. No one seemed too pleased when I pointed out that it had already been broadcast twice on radio! Certainly it wasn't felt necessary officiously to strive to

183

tell the public. Later it was turned into a successful stage play and subsequently produced once more for television, this time by a commercial company with Laurence Olivier in the lead.

My father was a very well-known divorce barrister. Instead of bed-time stories, 'Snow White' or whatever, he used to sit at the end of my bed and say, 'Today I managed to get costs against the co-respondent', or 'Today I managed to prove adultery by inclination and opportunity. An important part of the evidence was "footprints on the dashboard".' So early in my life it was decided that I should become a lawyer.

Legal anecdotes always seem to me rather cruel and although hilarious to judges and lawyers, those sentenced to death or long terms of imprisonment rarely join in the laughter. For example:

Judge. (to convicted murderer) Have you anything to say why sentence of death should not be passed against you?
Murderer. Damn all, my lord.
Judge. (to counsel) Mr Bleaks, did your client say something?
Mr Bleaks. Damn all, my Lord.
Judge. Funny, I could swear I heard him say something . . .

The main thing I have always found in the law is that the judge and the judged speak in different languages, coming as they do from different worlds. There used to be one exquisite judge at the Old Bailey – he always used to rise at 11.30 in the morning for a glass of Chablis and a nibble of Stilton, and he had to sentence a dead-drunk Irish labourer who'd assaulted the police, vomited down the stairs of Leicester Square Tube Station and appeared unshaven, red-eyed and staggering in the dock. This judge said, 'I'm going to take a most unusual course with you. A most merciful course. I'm going to place you on probation.'

'Oh, God bless you, your Honour. God bless your Royal Highness,' says the Irishman.

'But on one condition.'

'Anything, my Lord. Any condition, your Worship.'

'You're not to take another drink in your life.'

'Not a drop, I swear to your Holiness. Not a solitary drop.'

'And by that I mean absolutely *nothing*.' The judge leaned forward, smiling charmingly, 'Not even the *teeniest weeniest* little dry sherry before your dinner.'

So you see what I mean by the two different languages?

Far more interesting are the letters, diaries, the evidence of the accused. For instance, the Thompson/Bywaters case. Edith Thompson was an incurable romantic, a sort of Madame Bovary of Kensington Gardens. She fell in love with a young seaman, Bywaters, whom they say she induced to stab her husband to death. This is how she wrote to Frederick Bywaters:

Letter from Edith Thompson to Frederick Bywaters

On Thursday I went to the Waldorf for tea and while waiting in the vestibule by myself a gentleman came up, raised his hat and said, 'Are you Romance?' It seems he had an appointment with a lady he's corresponded with through the personal column . . .

I'm so stiff and sore today I can hardly move . . . This time last year you were able to rub me gradually and take that stiffness away. Do you remember?

It was rather fun on Thursday at the Garden Party. They had swings and roundabouts and flipflaps, coconut shies, Aunt Sallies, Hoopla, and all that sort of thing. I went in for them all and shocked a lot of people I think. I didn't care though. I'd got rather a posh frock on, white Georgette with rows and rows of jade ribbon and very white fur and large white hat, but all that didn't deter me from going into a fried fish shop in Snaresbrook and buying fish and chips. Getting it home was the worst part – it absolutely smelt the bus out. I didn't mind – it was rather fun – I only wish you had been with me. I think two halves would have enjoyed themselves, better than one half by herself.

Goodbye for now darlingest pal to Peidi.

Edith Bywaters and her lover were both hanged in 1923. But her love letters are better written than most judicial pronouncements.

When I was quite young my father went blind. As we lived near here, in the house I live in today, he used to travel up to London from Henley Station each day, and my mother had to read out all the evidence in his divorce cases to him. The First Class carriage on the Great Western would fall horribly silent as my mother read out accounts of private detectives peering through binoculars into strange bedrooms and seeing male and female clothing scattered around. But his being blind had two advantages for me. I used to read poetry aloud to him every night . . . to settle him down for sleep . . . And then he insisted on my writing myself so that we wouldn't run out of things to read . . . One of his favourite poets was Browning and I loved to read this poem because it is very musical and fun to read and because it speaks of an old dead romance which is still touching in the way that the romance of Bywaters and Thompson now is, perhaps, to us.

A Toccata of Galuppi's
ROBERT BROWNING

Oh, Galuppi, Baldassaro, this is very
    sad to find!
I can hardly misconceive you; it would
    prove me deaf and blind;
But although I take your meaning, 'tis
    with such a heavy mind!

Here you come with your old music,
    and here's all the good it brings.
What, they lived once thus in Venice
    where the merchants were the
    kings,
Where St Mark's is, where the Doges
    used to wed the sea with rings?

Ay, because the sea's the street there;
    and 'tis arched by . . . what you
    call
. . . Shylock's bridge with houses on it,
    where they kept the carnival:
I was never out of England – it's as if
    I saw it all!

Did young people take their pleasure
    when the sea was warm in May?
Balls and masks begun at midnight,

burning ever to mid-day
When they made up fresh adventures
for the morrow, do you say?

Was a lady such a lady, cheeks so
round and lips so red, –
On her neck the small face buoyant,
like a bell-flower on its bed,
O'er the breast's superb abundance
where a man might base his head?

Well (and it was graceful of them)
they'd break talk off and afford
– She, to bite her mask's black velvet –
he, to finger on his sword,
While you sat and played Toccatas,
stately at the clavichord?

What? Those lesser thirds so plaintive,
sixths diminished, sigh on
sigh,
Told them something? Those suspensions,
those solutions – 'Must we
die?'
Those commiserating sevenths – 'Life
might last! we can but try!'

'Were you happy?' – 'Yes.' 'And are
you still as happy?' – 'Yes. And
you?'
– 'Then, more kisses!' – 'Did I stop
them, when a million seemed so
few?'
Hark! the dominant's persistence, till
it must be answered to!

So an octave struck the answer. Oh,
they praised you, I dare say!
'Brave Galuppi! that was music! good
alike at grave and gay!
I can always leave off talking, when I
hear a master play.'

Then they left you for their pleasure:
    till in due time, one by one.
Some with lives that came to nothing,
    some with deeds as well undone.
Death came tacitly and took them
    where they never see the sun.

But when I sit down to reason, think
    to take my stand nor swerve,
While I triumph o'er a secret wrung
    from nature's close reserve,
In you come with your cold music, till
    I creep thro' every nerve.

Yes, you, like a ghostly cricket, creaking
    where a house was burned:
'Dust and ashes, dead and done with.
    Venice spent what Venice earned!
The soul, doubtless, is immortal –
    where a soul can be discerned.

As for Venice and its people, merely
    born to bloom and drop,
Here on earth they bore their fruitage,
    mirth and folly were the crop:
What of soul was left, I wonder, when
    the kissing had to stop?

'Dust and ashes!' So, you creak it,
    and I want the heart to scold.
Dear dead women, with such hair, too
    – what's become of all the gold
Used to hang and brush their bosoms?
    I feel chilly and grown old.

I have always loved, even adored, Lord Byron. We went to school together, at least his Turkish slippers were still in the library at Harrow and I lay on the tomb in the churchyard where he lay to write poetry. It's a place that now commands an excellent view of Ruislip and the gasworks. His Lordship's mixture of common sense and Romanticism, of conservatism and revolutionary fervour, of Puritanism and sensuality, are all exactly to my taste. Here he is observing an execution with true, lucid indifference and writing about it to John Murray:

Letter to John Murray
LORD BYRON
Venice, May 30th 1817

The day before I left Rome I saw three robbers guillotined. The ceremony – including the 'masqued' priests; the half-naked executioners; the bandaged criminals; the black Christ and his banner; the scaffold; the soldiery; the slow procession and the quick rattle and heavy fall of the axe; the splash of the blood, and the ghastliness of the exposed heads – is altogether more impressive than the vulgar and ungentlemanly dirty 'new drop', and dog-like agony of infliction upon the sufferers of the English sentence. Two of these men behaved calmly enough, but the first of the three died with great terror and reluctance, which was very horrible. He would not lie down; then his neck was too large for the aperture, and the priest was obliged to drown his exclamations by still louder exhortations. The head was off before the eye could trace the blow; but from an attempt to draw back the head, notwithstanding it was held forward by the hair, the first head was cut off close to the ears; the other two were taken off more cleanly. It is better than the oriental way, and (I should think) than the axe of our ancestors. The pain seems little; and yet the effect to the spectator, and the preparation to the criminal, are very striking and chilling. The first turned me quite hot and thirsty, and make me shake so that I could hardly hold the opera-glass (I was close, but determined to see, as one should see every thing, once, with attention); the second and third (which shows how dreadfully soon things grow indifferent) I am ashamed to say, had no effect on me as a horror, though I would have saved them if I could.

It is some time since I heard from you – the 12th April I believe. Yours Ever Truly,
B.

'My hand shook so that I could hardly hold the opera-glass', the perpetual attitude of the writer in the face of experience!

Readers: Jane Asher, Isobel Dean

Full Selection:
As I walked Out One Evening, W. H. AUDEN
Letter from Edith Thompson to Frederick Bywaters
A Toccata of Galuppi's, ROBERT BROWNING
The Myth of Sisyphus, ALBERT CAMUS
The Letters of Lord Byron
So We'll Go No More A'Roving, LORD BYRON
Seduced Girl, HEDYLOS trans. UNTERMAYER
Mr Youse Needn't be So Spry, E. E. CUMMINGS
As You Like It, Act 3, Scene 2, WILLIAM SHAKESPEARE
French Lisette: A Ballad of Maida Vale
The Taming of The Shrew, Act 5, Scene 2, WILLIAM SHAKESPEARE
The Way of the World, Act 4, Scene 5, WILLIAM CONGREVE
Waiting for the Barbarians, C. P. CAVAFY
The Possessed, DOSTOEVSKY
No Time to Go, E. E. CUMMINGS
Afterwards, THOMAS HARDY

DR DAVID OWEN

1985

Unlike many politicians David Owen was in fact born in the area for which he is Member of Parliament, Plymouth, and it was there we went to record the programme. His love of the place and its people was clear. Love of the sea has also exerted a powerful influence on his personality and was evident throughout his selection for the programme. His linking material was ad-libbed but, unusually for a politician, he was a man of few words.

190

Both my parents are Welsh. During the war my father was away fighting and of course Plymouth was savagely bombed so we went back to Wales and I spent some of my childhood there.

When I was quite small I developed a taste for going round graveyards and finding the rhymes on tombstones, such as this one from a Welsh cemetery:

> Here lies the body of Mary Jones
> Who died of eating cherry stones.
> Her name was Smith, it was not Jones,
> But Jones was put to rhyme with stones.

Another one I heard recently is:

> Here lies Solomon Peas under the trees and sod,
> But Peas is not here, only the pod;
> Peas shelled out and is gone to God.

We Devonians think Devon is the most beautiful county in England, but what is it that is so lovely? I think it's that part of Devon that lies between Dartmoor and the sea, and none lovelier than North Devon. This is an extract from a not very widely known book by Lawrence Whistler, *Initials in the Heart*, and it explains for me why Devon is an unmatched jewel.

Initials in the Heart
LAWRENCE WHISTLER

Between the valleys of the stream and the river, the deep and the deeper, the Halsdon ridge rose to a green brow with a wood on top, a landmark for miles. We began to know it as the Top of the World, the hyperbolical family name for a humbler knoll of my boyhood. From here extended westwards a view which I came to know like a face and love like a third person. It was a large view, though not large by the standards of mountain country – a semicircle of hilly distance that flowed from fluent Dartmoor about fifteen miles to the south, along the last high ground towards Cornwall, over flat tops and leafy knobs, grooved lanes roughly pointed towards hamlets, scattered white farms, and minute church-towers on skylines, round to Torrington spire, dead north; unexpected; a far sharp thought in a spireless composition. Towards that point the river dwindled in perspective, through a shaggy serpentine channel, hardly glimpsed. Engulfed immediately below us, it was quite unseen – but deeply understood – in the wide sweeps of its valley, whose funnelling walls were largely covered with woods cascading out of sight. From the pastures above they looked like overgrown amphitheatres of prodigious size, especially when a low sun put half into shadow, emphasizing the swerve of the fringed lip.

To many it might seem a very pleasant sample of pastoral England, hardly more. To me it was perfection; for it was secret and candid at once, wind-swept yet rich.

I'd like to read you a poem which was written by my greatest friend, Clive Grimson, who has since died sadly.

Once I Was Young
CLIVE GRIMSON

Once I was young
And filled with winged ideas
With songs unsung to echo down the years
The old man smiled
We sang those self same songs
Once on a time
Convinced we could right all wrongs
Thinking them blind
I kept my faith unfurled
Made up my mind
Youth would convert the world
The years have passed and I am older
Now
Youth does not last
The blossom leaves the bough
Yet wiser now I know a wider truth
I have learned how Hope is the
Spirit's youth.

I'm almost an adopted Londoner, having lived there ever since I was a medical student. I'd like to introduce to you 'The

Physician's Prayer' by Sir Robert Hutchison, a famous physician at the London Hospital. I might add that it would not be a
bad name for it to call it the 'Politician's Prayer'!

The Physician's Prayer
SIR ROBERT HUTCHISON

From inability to let well alone, from too much zeal for the new
and contempt for what is old, for putting knowledge before
wisdom, science before art and cleverness before common sense,
from treating patients as cases and for making the cure of the
disease more grievous than the endurance of the same, good
Lord deliver us.

Readers: Jane Asher, Peter Barkworth

Full Selection:
Drake's Drum, HENRY NEWBOLT
A Story, DYLAN THOMAS
Lepanto, G. K. CHESTERTON
Thou Shalt Dwell in Silence . . . , RABINDRANATH TAGORE
Solitude ELLA WHEELER WILCOX
Initials in the Heart, LAWRENCE WHISTLER
Candles, CAVAFY
Once I Was Young, CLIVE GRIMSON
The Ballad of Reading Gaol, OSCAR WILDE
They Who Are Near to Me, RABINDRANATH TAGORE
The Physician's Prayer, SIR ROBERT HUTCHISON
Business Girls, JOHN BETJEMAN
Body Remember, CAVAFY
The Hedgehog and The Fox, ISIAH BERLIN
Limerick, VICTOR GREY
Song by The Subconscious, Self, A. LANG
Adonais, P. B. SHELLEY
The Mary Gloster, RUDYARD KIPLING

JACQUELINE DU PRÉ

1980

About twenty years ago I was sent to a listening room in Broadcasting House to play back a tape of a concert which featured as soloist the then leader of the BBC Symphony Orchestra, Paul Beard. He was waiting when I arrived and I hurried to make everything ready. 'Don't rush,' he said. 'I'm expecting someone else.' At that moment Jacqueline du Pré breezed in, all good humour, long hair and youthful energy. I was so surprised and in awe that I could only blurt out 'Hello. I've just bought one of your records.'

'Oh really,' said Paul Beard. 'Was it any good?'

The conversation between them was full of such banter. The music, when they finally allowed me to play the tape, was exquisite. The regard they had for each other was evident in the quality of the listening. Eventually, the concert over, she had to leave, watched admiringly by both of us. Even though she hadn't played a note, it was as if she had taken the music with her.

One day, when I was four, I was in the kitchen, bored to tears. We had an old-fashioned wireless and I climbed over the ironing board and switched it on. There was a programme – some sort of illustration of the instruments of the orchestra. I didn't like it 'till I heard the cello and I said, 'I want to play that sound.' And so I was given a cello.

I woke up and found this whopping creature beside my bed. Plucking it made a nice sound. I got out of bed and put it between my legs – I'd never seen anyone playing before. I loved it, kept going back to it. I had heard somewhere: 'A noise rose from the orchestra as the leader drew across the intestines of the timid cat, the tail of the noble horse.' I remember being desperately inspired by the idea of horse hair and catgut getting married to make that lovely sound – the bow is made of horse hair, white horse hair, and the strings are made of catgut – actually it's sheep's gut, but don't tell anyone.

We lived in Purley. However, I ran away when I was three. I was away from 7 a.m. to 7.30 p.m. and the Surrey police were alerted. It was panic stations. 'Where have you been?'

'I've been to sea, of course.'

Although how I could possibly have gone to the sea from Purley, I can't imagine. I think it was pretty beastly personally. I did it again when I was five – on my tricycle.

'Where have you been?'

'I've been to Brighton.'

Since I've been talking about the sea, this poem can remind us of the smell of the sea, one of the poems I remember hearing my sister Hilary reciting as part of her elocution lessons.

Cargoes
JOHN MASEFIELD

Quinquireme of Nineveh from distant Ophir
Rowing home to haven in sunny Palestine,
With a cargo of ivory,
And apes and peacocks,
Sandalwood, cedarwood, and sweet white wine.

Stately Spanish galleon coming from the Isthmus,
Dipping through the Tropics by the palm-green shores,
With a cargo of diamonds,
Emeralds, amethysts,
Topazes, and cinnamon, and gold moidores.

Dirty British coaster with a salt-caked smoke stack
Butting through the Channel in the mad March days,
With a cargo of Tyne coal,
Road-rail, pig-lead,
Firewood, iron-ware, and cheap tin trays.

I went in for a competition when I was ten and won it, which meant that I had to practise at least four hours a day. (I cut it down to as few as I could because I couldn't stand practising!) It meant that I had to leave school – to me, in fact, it was a golden day. It did, however, mean that I didn't come into contact with other children.

My family moved to Portland Place where my father took up some accountancy work. Father had a stick insect – bless its heart. I couldn't find a way to love it, and I hated it. She was christened Amanda, Mandy for short, and lived in her own aquarium. When she died she was given a burial in Regent's Park, and the deeply religious service was conducted by my father. He still remembers the place which marks the spot where Amanda lies. Thank goodness stick insects didn't have a prolonged stay. I did have a budgie and I know that humming-birds took my fancy as well.

Humming-Bird
D. H. LAWRENCE

I can imagine, in some other world
Primeval-dumb, far back
In that most awful stillness, that only gasped and
    hummed,
Humming-birds raced down the avenues.

Before anything had a soul,
While life was a heave of Matter, half inanimate,
This little bit chipped off in brilliance
And went whizzing through the slow, vast, succulent
    stems.

I believe there were no flowers then,
In the world where the humming-bird flashed ahead of
    creation.
I believe he pierced the slow vegetable veins with his
    long beak.

Probably he was big
As mosses, and little lizards, they say, were once big.
Probably he was a jabbing, terrifying monster.

196

> We look at him through the wrong end of the long
> telescope of Time,
> Luckily for us.

It was fortunate that we lived near Regent's Park, because it meant that, when I was fed up with practising, I could escape and be as wild as I liked, surrounded by all the things I loved, like trees and flowers. Regent's Park has been full of daffodils while we have been preparing this programme. I told John Carson (*the reader, with Penelope Lee, of most of the items in this programme*) that Wordsworth's 'Daffodils' was one of my favourites. He couldn't pick any in the park and the shops were shut on the following evening when we met, so he offered me this sentimental verse instead – written by the most famous poet in the world, Anon.

> 'Thank you for the flowers you sent,' she said,
> And sweetly smiled and coyly turned her head
> 'I'm sorry for the things I said last night.
> I was wrong and you were right,
> Please forgive me.'
> So I forgave her. And as we wandered through the
> moonlit hours
> I thought, 'What bloody flowers?'

Everybody knows, I think, what it's like to have the giggles and they can be quite devastating when you are trying to do something very smooth and controlled, like playing 'The Swan'. Perhaps you can imagine how difficult it is to hold a legato line when your body is dancing a wild tango inside. I certainly giggled during other bits of 'Carnival of the Animals'.

The Fossils from The Carnival of the Animals
OGDEN NASH

> At midnight in the museum hall
> The fossils gathered for a ball.
> There were no drums or saxophones
> But just the clatter of their bones,
> A rolling, rattling, carefree circus
> Of mammoth polkas and mazurkas.
> Pterodactyls and brontosauruses

> Sang ghostly prehistoric choruses
> Amid the mastodonic wassail
> I caught the eye of one small fossil.
> Cheer up, sad world, he said, and winked –
> It's kind of fun to be extinct.

Elgar is certainly not fossilised, especially in our hearts. I found in this book of things I'd written:

Elgar's photo now hangs on the wall – a document which tells so vividly of his unhappy life. A sick man who had through it a glowing heart in such a profusion of loveliness as expressed in so many of his works. How his face haunts me, and always will.

These are other short observations which I found in my book:

Never mind about present affliction – any moment may be the next!

I suppose all of us must learn to find independence in dependence.

If the sunshine beckons you, accept its invitation and love the gold quality of it.

Genius is one who, with an innate capacity, affects for good or evil, the life of others.

Don't let the sound of your own wheels drive you crazy.

A relationship is not that you would like it to be – or what you think it is. It defines *itself* by the actual quality of the interchange between the people involved.

This is called 'A Persian Apothegm'

> He who knows not and knows not that he knows not
>   is a fool – shun him
> He who knows not and knows that he knows not
>   can be taught – teach him
> He who knows and knows not that he knows
>   is asleep – wake him
> He who knows and knows that he knows
>   is a prophet – follow him

This is about the reading of 'Peter and the Wolf' from an actress friend:

Don't over emotionalise the wording, the music is there to illustrate the words.

It occurred to me that this is what I want to convey to my pupils – that the expression is inbuilt in the music and shape of the piece as well. Too much expressive indulgence will distort the musical structure.

I was always a lover, since childhood, of the winter elements – of snow as it graced the earth gently with its snowdrops leaving that pristine white carpet. Oh what a shame to spoil its velvet smoothness with a common footprint, but what a delicious excitement to create evidence of one's exploration into a virgin land. I remember the search for the single, magically designed snowflake, or of flinging myself into the snow, loving its texture, the cold against one's skin and the fun of constructing hard snowballs to throw at random to watch their passage through the air and then their splintering rebound on the chosen target.

Wind and rain also thrilled me, as the first would dance wildly through my hair, buffeting my cheeks, exciting them to warmth, and also induce beauteous scents, and the second with its pitter-patter which would invite the imagination to new worlds, would bathe flowers into which I could explore the moisture with my face embedded in them, and the thrill with the luscious scents the rain would invite into my world.

Written at 2 a.m. when my mind feels somewhat muddy and I have never been much of a mud lover!

When I went to receive a doctorate from London University presented by the Queen Mother, the oration was read by Professor John Barron. At the end he read the last verse of Wordsworth's 'The Solitary Reaper'.

The Solitary Reaper
WILLIAM WORDSWORTH

Whate'er the theme, the Maiden sang
As if her song could have no ending;

I saw her singing at her work,
   And o'er the sickle bending;
I listen'd, motionless and still;
And, as I mounted up the hill,
The music in my heart I bore,
Long after it was heard no more.

Readers: John Carson, Penelope Lee

Full Selection:
Romance, W. J. TURNER
Cargoes, JOHN MASEFIELD
Humming-Bird, D. H. LAWRENCE
Inversnaid, GERARD MANLEY HOPKINS
Thank You for the Flowers . . . , ANON
Heaven, RUPERT BROOKE
Fish for Luncheon, HERBERT FARJEON
The Solitary Reaper, WILLIAM WORDSWORTH
The Fossils from *Carnival of the Animals,* OGDEN NASH
A Persian Apothegm
Love's Labour's Lost, WILLIAM SHAKESPEARE
To Autumn, JOHN KEATS
To the Gentlemen in Row D, VIRGINIA GRAHAM
The Listeners, WALTER DE LA MARE
The Tiger, WILLIAM BLAKE
Snake, D. H. LAWRENCE
Museum Piece, RICHARD WILBUR
The English Are So Nice!, D. H. LAWRENCE
Lies, YEVGENY YEVTUSHENKO
Vote for Love and *God Bless Love,* complied by NANETTE NEWMAN
Searching for Love, D. H. LAWRENCE

STEVE RACE

1971

'With Great Pleasure' is one of those programmes that has a repeat broadcast within the week of its first transmission. Due to some administrative quirk, however, Steve's edition did not get its second airing. I am hoping to repair that omission in the near future, but in the meantime, it gives me great pleasure to include some of the script here. Steve has managed to combine the career of a successful musician with that of a successful broadcaster. Indeed, in my early days of playing the records in such programmes as 'Housewives Choice', which he used to present regularly along with many others, he struck me as one of the disconcertingly few people in broadcasting who really knew what he was doing. My estimation of the others has grown kinder with experience, but the professionalism, ease and clarity of expression which Steve displayed and continues to display remain a model that many broadcasters could strive to emulate.

105 years ago a relative on my father's side received through the post a proposal of marriage. She was Mary Foster, of Middlemoor, Pateley Bridge in Yorkshire, and she was the local beauty. The letter of proposal she received *is* genuine: my family has the original. The letter certainly was (as the writer said) 'in desprit and yurnest'.

Hopeful Proposal to a Young Lady of the Village,
Dated November 29th, 1866

My Dear Miss,
      I now take up my pen to write to you hoping these few

lines will find you well as it leaves me at present Thank God for it. You will perhaps be surprised that I should make so bold as to write to you who is such a lady and I hope you will not be vex at me for it. I hardly dare say what I want, I am so timid about ladies, and my heart trimmels like a hespin. But I once seed in a book that faint heart never won fair lady, so here goes.

I am a farmer in a small way and my age is rather more than forty years and my mother lives with me and keeps my house, and she has been very poorly lately and cannot stir about much and I think I should be more comfortabler with a wife.

I have had my eye on you a long time and I think you are a very nice young woman and one that would make me happy if only you think so. We keep a servant girl to milk three kye and do the work in the house, and she goes out a bit in the summer to gadder wickens and she snags a few of turnips in the back kend. I do a piece of work on the farm myself and attends Pately Market, and I sometimes show a few sheep and I feeds between 3 & 4 pigs agen Christmas, and the same is very useful in the house to make pies and cakes and so forth, and I sells the hams to help pay for the barley meal.

I have about 73 pund in Naisbro Bank and we have a nice little parlour downstairs with a blue carpet, and an oven on the side of the fireplace and the old woman on the other side smoking. The Golden Rules claimed up on the walls above the long settle, and you could sit all day in the easy chair and knit and mend my kytles and leggums, and you could make the tea ready agin I come in, and you could make butter for Pately Market, and I would drive you to church every Sunday in the spring cart, and I would do all that bees in my power to make you happy. So I hope to hear from you. I am in desprit and Yurnest, and will marry you at May Day, or if my mother dies afore I shall want you afore. If only you will accept of me, my dear, we could be very happy together.

I hope you will let me know your mind by return of post, and if you are favourable I will come up to scratch. So no more at present from your well-wisher and true love –
Simon Fallowfield

P.S. I hope you will say nothing about this. If you will not accept of me I have another very nice woman in my eye, and I think I shall marry her if you do not accept of me, but I thought you would suit me mother better, she being very crusty at times. So I tell you now before you come, she will be Maister.

No, she didn't marry him, but I hope some nice girl did.

Up in Weardale, County Durham, lie the bones of my ancestors. They came from Weardale and Teesdale for 300 years; before that, from South Yorkshire, back to 1386, when John Race, of Beverley, leased some land and put his name to a deed.

So it's not surprising that the Dales are in my blood. My father – a young man growing up in the Durham dales – used to tramp over the fells with a friend called Fred G. Bowles. That was about the turn of the century, and there's a family story that one sweltering hot day Fred Bowles shed first his coat, then eventually his trousers, slinging them over his shoulder and tramping on across the deserted moors; until at last they came to a little town and Fred discovered that his trousers must have slipped off his shoulder . . . Anyway, all he had was a jacket.

Fred G. Bowles was a fine, if now unremembered poet.

Resurrection
FRED G. BOWLES

As the slow evening gathered in her grey
And one clear star its ancient pathway trod,
With long, low cadences of clear delay
The lark, descending, left his song with God.
And peace came, like a reverential soul,
With far-off tremors of a further world,
And through the silver mist of twilight, stole
Into the heart of all. And upward curled
The April moon, resurgent of the sun,
To the blue dust of the exalted dome
Of heaven; and the white wind-flowers, one by one,
Shook in light slumber on their hilly home.
It was so sweet to stoop, and feel around! –
Each blade of grass a breathing lyre of life
Whereon the wind, in arias of sound,
Told subtle music; how the great world, rife
With scent of violets and primrose-strewn,

Strained tender fingers from each dewy sod
To the dear Christ of chrysalis and moon.
And dusk, descending, left her soul with God.

There are some people – kindred spirits – whom one positively *hugs* across the centuries. For me, one of these is the Reverend Sydney Smith, born in 1771. He was a great humanitarian, the most famous wit of his day, and a darling man. Consider this letter he wrote to a little girl:

Lucy, dear child,
Mind your arithmetic. You know, in the first sum of yours I ever saw, there was a mistake. You had carried two (as a cab is licensed to do) and you ought, dear Lucy, to have carried one. Is this a trifle? What would life be, without arithmetic, but a scene of horrors? . . . I now give you my parting advice: don't marry anybody who has not a tolerable understanding and a thousand a year. God bless you, dear child.

Sydney Smith, though himself a Canon of St Paul's, found senior churchmen irresistibly funny. Describing the scene when the Church Commissioners were at last compelled by the Home Secretary of the day to yield some of their property to its rightful owners, he wrote:

The Commission was separated in an instant. London clenched his fist; Canterbury was hurried out by his chaplains and put in a warm bed; a solemn vacancy spread itself over the face of Gloucester; Lincoln was taken out in strong hysterics.

When Lady Grey wrote to Sidney Smith angrily demanding his support for declaring war against Denmark, he replied:

My Dear Lady Grey:
For God's sake do not drag me into another war! I am worn down and worn out with crusading and defending Europe and protecting mankind: I *must* think a little of myself. I am sorry for the Spaniards – I am sorry for the Greeks – I deplore the fate of the Jews – the people of the Sandwich Islands are groaning under the most detestable tyranny – Bagdad is oppressed – I do not

like the present state of the Delta – Tibet is not comfortable. Am I to fight for all these people? The world is bursting with sin and sorrow.

No war, dear Lady Grey! No eloquence; but apathy, selfishness, commonsense, arithmetic. I will go to war with the King of Denmark if he is impertinent to you, but for no other cause.

More than Jingoists, more than Bishops, Sidney Smith disdained Politicians. Here he's describing William Pitt, the parliamentary spellbinder of his day.

He was one of the most luminous, eloquent blunderers with which any people was ever afflicted. For 15 years I have found my income dwindling away under his eloquence, and regularly in every session of Parliament he has charmed every classical feeling and stript me of every guinea I possessed. At the close of every brilliant display, an expedition failed or a Kingdom fell. By the time that his style had gained the summit of perfection, Europe was degraded to the lowest abyss of misery. God send us a stammerer; a tongueless man!

John Evelyn was a civil servant; a gardener; a diarist. He was a family man, living in Surrey and later near Deptford, and he left a description of his small son which I find almost unbelievable, and most touching.

John Evelyn's Diary
Entry for 27 January 1658

After six fits of a quartan ague with which it pleased God to visit him, died my dear son Richard, to our inexpressible grief and affliction, five years and three days old only, but at that tender age a prodigy for wit and understanding; for beauty of body a very angel; for endowment of mind of incredible and rare hopes. To give only a little taste of them, and thereby glory to God, he hath learnt all his catechism; at two years and a half old he could perfectly read any of the English, Latin, French or Gothic letters, pronouncing the first three languages exactly. He had before the fifth year not only skill to read most written hands, but to decline all nouns, conjugate the verbs regular and most of the irregular;

learnt 'Puerilis', got by heart almost the entire vocabulary of Latin and French primitives and words, could make congruous syntax, turn English into Latin and vice versa, construe and prove what he read, knew the government and use of relatives, verbs, substantives, ellipses and many figures and tropes, began himself to write legibly and had a strong passion for Greek.

The number of verses he could write was prodigious; he remembered the parts of plays, which he would also act. Seeing a Plautus in one's hand, he asked what book it was, and being told it was comedy and too difficult for him, he wept for sorrow. Strange was his apt and ingenious application of fables and morals, for he had read Aesop. He had a wonderful disposition for mathematics, having by heart divers propositions of Euclid that we read to him in play. As to his piety, astonishing were his applications of Scripture on occasion. He had learnt all his Catechism early, and understood the historical part of the Bible and New Testament to a wonder.

These, and like illuminations far exceeding his age and experience, considering the prettiness of his address and behaviour, cannot but leave impressions in me at the memory of him. He would of himself select the most pathetic psalms and chapters out of Job to read to his maid during his sickness, telling her, when she pitied him, that all God's children must suffer affliction. He declaimed against the vanities of the world before he had seen any. How thankfully he would receive admonition! – How soon be reconciled! How indifferent, yet continually cheerful! He would give grave advice to his brother John, bear with his impertinences, and say he was but a child. He was all life, all prettiness; far from morose, sullen or childish in anything he said or did.

The day before he died he called to me, and in a more serious manner than usual, told me that for all I loved him so dearly, I should give my house, land and all my fine things to his brother Jack.

Next morning, when he found himself ill, and I persuaded him to keep his hands in bed, he demanded whether he might pray to God with his hands unjoined. A little after, whilst in great agony, he asked whether he should not offend God by using his only name so often calling for ease.

But thus God, having dressed up a saint fit for himself, would no longer permit him with us, unworthy of the future fruits of this incomparable hopeful blossom. Such a child I never saw, for such a child I bless God, in whose bosom he is. Thou gavest him to us, thou hast taken him away from us: blessed be the name of the Lord!

In my opinion he was suffocated by the women and maids who attended him, and covered him too hot with blankets as he lay in his cradle, near an excessive hot fire in a closed room.

Here ends the joy of my life, and for which I go ever mourning to the grave.

15 February
The afflicting hand of God being still upon us, it pleased him also to take away from us this morning my youngest son, George, now seven weeks languishing at nurse and ending in a dropsy. God's holy will be done.

Readers: Prunella Scales, Timothy West

Full Selection:
Painting as a Pastime, SIR WINSTON CHURCHILL
At Grass, PHILIP LARKIN
A Discreet Immorality, JOHN SMITH
Boswell's Life of Johnson
Remember, CHRISTINA ROSSETTI
Jack Mytton, VIRGINIA WOOLF
Resurrection, FRED G. BOWLES
Quotations from Sydney Smith
Why I Love England, MALCOLM MUGGERIDGE
Diary of John Evelyn
When You Are Old, W. B. YEATS
The Caraway Seed, OGDEN NASH
The Fly, OGDEN NASH
The Bat, OGDEN NASH
The Pizza, OGDEN NASH
Crossing the Border, OGDEN NASH
Civilisation, A Personal View, KENNETH CLARK

DIANA RIGG

1978

This excellent and attractive actress took on the task of compiling her programme with gusto. The range of people and literary styles included was wide, from John Wilmot, Earl of Rochester, to Freud – no doubt the latter would have had something to say about the former, but his words were intercut with an amusing poem mischievously celebrating physical love, thereby rendering him, at a stroke as it were, pompous and puzzled. In fact Diana Rigg's especial pleasure was in storytelling, and it was that which led her to her profession. By storytelling she meant not just the tale being told, but the excitement of the words themselves, 'finding a private interpretation fed by the sounds and one's imagination'.

Whilst going through my books for this programme I came across an old half-crown edition of antonyms and synonyms. Twenty-five years ago I underlined certain words, words which now remind me of the conflict and pain of being teen-aged – bewilder, envenomed, forswear, grapple, impotent, mortal, mutinous, secret, waggish, void. The void was always guaranteed to be filled.

Sonnets from the Portuguese
ELIZABETH BARRETT BROWNING

I lived with visions for my company,
Instead of men and women, years ago,
And found them gentle mates, nor thought to know
A sweeter music than they played to me.

But soon their trailing purple was not free
Of this world's dust, – their lutes did silent grow,
And I myself grew faint and blind below
Their vanishing eyes. Then THOU didst come . . . to be,
Beloved, what they seemed. Their shining fronts,
Their songs, their splendours, (better, yet the same,
As river-water hallowed into fonts)
Met in thee, and from out thee overcame
My soul with satisfaction of all wants –
Because God's gifts put man's best dreams to shame.

But if you happen to be a lumpish fourteen-year old, a God's gift wasn't likely to appear, nor indeed if he had would one have known what to do with him. An older man was the classic answer, but perhaps the next poem was going a tidge too far.

A Song of a Young Lady to Her Ancient Lover
JOHN WILMOT, EARL OF ROCHESTER

Ancient Person, for whom I
All the flattering youth defy;
Long be it e're thou grow old,
Aching, shaking, crazy, cold.
But still continue as thou art,
Ancient Person of my Heart.

On thy withered lips and dry,
Which like barren furrows lie;
Brooding kisses I will pour,
Shall thy youthful heart restore.
Such kind show'rs in autumn fall,
And a second spring recall:
Nor from thee will ever part,
Ancient Person of my Heart.

All a lover's wish can reach,
For thy joy my love shall teach:
And for thy pleasure shall improve
All that art can add to love.
Yet still I love thee without art,
Ancient Person of my Heart.

I was deeply shocked on reading this next poem. I still am but for different reasons. Its overt sexuality was gross when I compared it to the softer, more abstract visions of women I'd hitherto encountered and the symbolism which runs through it disturbed my prosaic consciousness.

Figs
D. H. LAWRENCE

The proper way to eat a fig in society,
Is to split it in four, holding it by the stump,
And open it, so that it is a glittering, rosy, moist,
    honied, heavy-petalled four-petalled flower.
Then you throw away the skin
Which is just like a four-sepalled calyx,
After you have taken off the blossom with your lips.

But the vulgar way
Is just to put your mouth to the crack, and take out the
    flesh in one bite.

Every fruit has its secret.

The fig is a very secretive fruit.
As you see it standing growing, you feel at once it is
    symbolic:
And it seems male.
But when you come to know it better, you agree with
    the Romans, it is female.

The Italians vulgarly say, it stands for the female part;
    the fig fruit:
The fissure, the yoni,
The wonderful moist conductivity towards the centre.

Involved,
Inturned,
The flowering all inward and womb-fibrilled;
And but one orifice.

The fig, the horse-shoe, the squash blossom.
Symbols.

There was a flower that flowered inward, womb-ward;
Now there is a fruit like a ripe womb.

It was always a secret.
That's how it should be, the female should always be
    secret.

There never was any standing aloft and unfolded on a
    bough
Like other flowers, in a revelation of petals;
Silver-pink peach, Venetian green glass of medlars and
    sorb-apples,
Shallow wine-cups on short, bulging stems
Openly pledging heaven:
Here's to the thorn in flower! Here is to utterance!
The brave, adventurous rosaceae.

Foiled upon itself, and secret unutterable,
The milky-sapped, sap that curdles milk and makes
    ricotta,
Sap that smells strange on your fingers, that even goats
    won't taste it;
Folded upon itself, enclosed like any Mohammedan
    woman,
Its nakedness all within-walls, its flowering forever
    unseen,
One small way of access only, and this close-curtained
    from the light;

Fig, fruit of the female mystery, covert and inward,
Mediterranean fruit, with your covert nakedness,
Where everything happens invisible, flowering and
    fertilization, and fruiting
In the inwardness of you, that eye will never see
Till it's finished, and you're over-ripe, and you burst to
    give up your ghost.

Till the drop of ripeness exudes,
And the year is over.

And then the fig has kept her secret long enough.
So it explodes and you see through the fissure the scarlet.

211

And the fig is finished, the year is over.

That's how the fig dies, showing her crimson through
    the purple slit.
Like a wound, the exposure of her secret, on the open
    day.
Like a prostitute, the bursten fig, making a show of
    her secret.

That's how women die too.

The year is fallen over-ripe,
The year of our women.
The year of our women is fallen over-ripe.
The secret is laid bare.
And rottenness soon sets in.
The year of our women is fallen over-ripe.

When Eve once knew in her mind that she was naked
She quickly sewed fig-leaves, and sewed the same for
    man.
She'd been naked all her days before,
But till then, till that apple of knowledge, she hadn't
    had the fact on her mind.

She got the fact on her mind, and quickly sewed fig
    leaves.
And women have been sewing ever since.
But now they stitch to adorn the bursten fig, not to
    cover it.
They have their nakedness more than ever on their
    mind,
And they won't let us forget it.

Now the secret
Becomes an affirmation through moist, scarlet lips
That laugh at the Lord's indignation.

What then good Lord! cry the women.
We have kept our secret long enough.
We are a ripe fig.
Let us burst in affirmation.

They forget, ripe figs won't keep.
Ripe figs won't keep.
Honey-white figs of the north, black figs with scarlet
  inside, of the south.
Ripe figs won't keep, won't keep in any clime.
What then, when women the world over have all
  bursten into self-assertion?
And bursten figs won't keep?

Mr Lawrence must be gyrating in his grave at the self-assertion of
women today and I can't help adding that it serves him right!

Readers: Philip Voss, Diana Rigg

Full Selection:
You English Words, JOHN MOORE
The Birth of the Rune from the Finnish
Jabberwocky, LEWIS CARROLL
How the Whale got His Throat, RUDYARD KIPLING
Romance, W. J. TURNER
The Listeners, WALTER DE LA MARE
Sonnets from the Portuguese, ELIZABETH BARRETT BROWNING
A Song from a Young Lady to Her Ancient Lover, JOHN WILMOT,
EARL OF ROCHESTER
Figs, D. H. LAWRENCE
When I was Young and Fair, ELIZABETH I
The Hollow Crown comp. JOHN BARTON
Compilation: Young Corydon and Phyllis/Freud
Check to Song, OWEN MEREDITH
Poet in the Making, DYLAN THOMAS
Poetry, YEVGENY YEVTUSHENKO
Lullaby, W. H. AUDEN

HARRY SECOMBE

1975

It is frequently said of comedians that they conceal personalities well on the dismal side of gloomy. My own, fairly limited, experience of working with them leads me to the conclusion that this is only occasionally true and that funny men who are otherwise depressed are bound to be remarked upon. The remainder have as wide a range of off-stage personalities as any other group. However, there are neuroses and insecurities peculiar to that occupation: the fear of not being funny in front of maybe hundreds of people who have paid to see them being just that; the nagging feeling that after years of being successful it is not quite right that they remain merely an object of laughter – even though the pleasure of the audience is obvious, there must be a wish occasionally to say something without having people doubling up. I've met Harry Secombe in a studio only once and he was most entertaining. He clearly enjoyed giving pleasure and appeared withal a warm and genuinely friendly person. It was no surprise to read his 'With Great Pleasure' script and find a sensitive and thoughtful person amongst the jokes.

As Wales contains some of the wildest, highest and most beautiful country in the British Isles, it's not surprising that the Welsh love nature poetry, even when it's written by an Englishman.

A favourite scene in nature is a lake, under a grey sky with a chill wind rippling the water and rustling the reeds, and the wild ducks flying. The awful loneliness of such a scene at evening, especially in late autumn, is brought to mind by extracts from John Masefield's passion play in verse, 'Good Friday'. I've chosen this because it was my first appearance in a play ever – in the church hall, of course. I was 14 years old and made up as an old blind beggar, covered in grey crêpe hair, which made speech rather difficult. I'm afraid I haven't got that excuse today.

Good Friday
JOHN MASEFIELD

The wild duck, stringing through the sky,
Are south away.
Their green necks glitter as they fly,
The lake is gray.
So still, so lone, the fowler never heeds.
The wind goes rustle, rustle, through the reeds.

There they find peace to have their own wild souls.
In that still lake,
Only the moonrise or the wind controls
The way they take,
Through the gray reeds, the cocking moor-hen's lair,
Rippling the pool, or over leagues of air.

Not thus, not thus are the wild souls of men.
No peace for those
Who step beyond the blindness of the pen
To where the skies unclose.
For them the spitting mob, the cross, the crown of thorns
The bull gone mad, the Saviour on his horns.

I first discovered Keats when I was about 14 – the time when people usually start writing that terrible adolescent romantic verse, and I was no exception. I thought in Keats that I'd found a kindred spirit, and in fact I was so affected by Keats' life and work that by the time I was 15 I was sure I had all the symptoms of TB. This poem is the first Keats poem I ever read.

Ode to Autumn
JOHN KEATS

Season of mists and mellow fruitfulness,
   Close bosom-friend of the maturing sun;
Conspiring with him how to load and bless
   With fruit the vines that round the thatch-eaves run;

To bend with apples the moss'd cottage-trees,
    And fill all fruit with ripeness to the core;
       To swell the gourd, and plump the hazel shells
With a sweet kernel; to set budding more,
    And still more, later flowers for the bees,
    Until they think warm days will never cease,
       For Summer has o'er-brimm'd their clammy cells.

Who hath not seen thee oft amid thy store?
    Sometimes whoever seeks abroad may find
Thee sitting careless on a granary floor,
    Thy hair soft-lifted by the winnowing wind;
Or on a half-reap'd furrow sound asleep,
    Drowsed with the fume of poppies, while thy hook
      Spares the next swath and all its twined flowers:
And sometimes like a gleaner thou dost keep
    Steady thy laden head across a brook;
    Or by a cider-press, with patient look,
      Thou watchest the last oozings, hours by hours.

Where are the songs of Spring? Aye, where are they?
    Think not of them, thou hast thy music too, –
While barred clouds bloom the soft-dying day,
    And touch the stubble-plains with rosy hue;
Then in a wailful choir the small gnats mourn
    Among the river sallows, borne aloft
      Or sinking as the light wind lives or dies;
And full-grown lambs loud bleat from hilly bourn;
    Hedge-crickets sing; and now with treble soft
    The red-breast whistles from a garden croft;
      And gathering swallows twitter in the skies.

After a year or two as a clerk in the colliery office, I joined the Territorial Army – not strictly out of patriotism, I may say, but because all the other clerks in the office joined the same Territorial Regiment which meant that when they all went off together to camp for two weeks I was left to do all the work, so, being rather clever, I put my age on by two years and joined up myself: went off to camp gaily in August 1939 and returned home in April 1946. Some fool had declared war in between. They say that a soldier can find a Field-Marshal's baton in his knapsack – well I went to war with Palgrave's *Golden Treasury* in mine for certain reasons, I mean shrapnel and other things coming over I could always place it in a strategic position. Today I'd need *Encyclopedia Britannica*. But after the war I took to reading much of the poetry left by the authors of the First World War; having been in a war myself, I wanted to see what they thought about it: Siegfried Sassoon, Edmund Blunden, Robert Graves and especially the Welsh poet, Wilfred Owen, but of course it was Rupert Brooke who helped set the mood of romantic patriotism that was so popular during the early days of the First World War.

The Soldier
RUPERT BROOKE

If I should die, think only this of me:
   That there's some corner of a foreign field
That is for ever England. There shall be
   In that rich earth a richer dust concealed;
A dust whom England bore, shaped, made aware,
   Gave, once, her flowers to love, her ways to roam,
A body of England's, breathing English air,
   Washed by the rivers, blest by suns of home.

And think, this heart, all evil shed away,
   A pulse in the eternal mind, no less
      Gives somewhere back the thoughts by England given;
Her sights and sounds; dreams happy as her day;
   And laughter, learnt of friends; and gentleness,
      In hearts at peace, under an English heaven.

Rupert Brooke did die abroad, from malaria, but it was a hero's death, he was bitten by a German mosquito. He was buried in some foreign field and never knew how the war had changed from romantic patriotism into bitter disillusion. Compare Brooke's 'Soldier' with Siegfried Sassoon's 'Suicide in the Trenches'.

Suicide in the Trenches
SIEGFRIED SASSOON

I knew a simple soldier boy
Who grinned at life in empty joy,

217

Slept soundly throught the lonesome dark,
And whistled early with the lark.

In winter trenches, cowed and glum,
With crumps and lice and lack of rum,
He put a bullet through his brain.
No one spoke of him again.

You smug-faced crowds with kindling eye
Who cheer when soldier lads march by,
Sneak home and pray you'll never know
The hell where youth and laughter go.

The Welsh poet, Wilfred Owen who was killed in battle in 1918 just before the Armistice, had said of his poems 'The subject is war and the pity of war' which is what attracts me to the writings of most of those First World War poets. They saw war for what it really was, mud, death, stink and filth, not a flag-waving, jingoist adventure as so many of the folks at home saw it. Here is Wilfred Owen's 'Dulce et Decorum Est' – How sweet to die for one's country – or is it?

Dulce et Decorum Est
WILFRED OWEN

Bent double, like old beggars under sacks,
Knock-kneed, coughing like hags, we cursed through sludge,
Till on the haunting flares we turned our backs
And towards our distant rest began to trudge.
Men marched asleep. Many lost their boots
But limped on, blood-shod. All went lame; all blind;
Drunk with fatigue; deaf even to the hoots
Of tired, outstripped Five-Nines that dropped behind.

Gas! GAS! Quick, boys! – An ecstacy of fumbling,
Fitting the clumsy helmets just in time;
But someone still was yelling out and stumbling
And floud'ring like a man in fire or lime . . .
Dim, through the misty panes and thick green light,
As under a green sea, I saw him drowning.

In all my dreams, before my helpless sight,
He plunges at me, guttering, choking, drowning.

If in some smothering dreams you too could pace
Behind the wagon that we flung him in,
And watch the white eyes writhing in his face,
His hanging face, like a devil's sick of sin;
If you could hear, at every jolt, the blood
Come gargling from the froth-corrupted lungs,
Obscene as cancer, bitter as the cud
Of vile, incurable sores on innocent tongues, –
My friend, you would not tell with such high zest
To children ardent for some desperate glory,
The old Lie: Dulce et decorum est
Pro patria mori.

Readers: Andrew Secombe, Harry Secombe

Full Selection:
The Days that Have Been, W. H. DAVIES
Portrait of the Artist as a Young Dog, DYLAN THOMAS
The Collier, VERNON WATKINS
Fern Hill, DYLAN THOMAS
Madly in All Directions, WYNFORD VAUGHAN THOMAS
Good Friday, JOHN MASEFIELD
Ode to Autumn, JOHN KEATS
The Soldier, RUPERT BROOKE
Suicide in the Trenches, SIEGFRIED SASSOON
Dulce et Decorum Est, WILFRED OWEN
The Return, WILFRED GIBSON
Raining, WILFRED GIBSON
The Death of the Queen, WILLIAM MCGONAGALL
Fear No More the Heat of the Sun from *Cymbeline,* WILLIAM
SHAKESPEARE
The Calf, OGDEN NASH
Listen, OGDEN NASH
The Rabbits, OGDEN NASH

Faithless Nellie Gray, THOMAS HOOD
The Pickwick Papers, CHARLES DICKENS
In Focus, JEREMY ROBSON
The Children of Aberfan, SPIKE MILLIGAN

NED SHERRIN

1970

It is current fashion to dismiss the sixties as a decade of frivolity and profligacy, a celebration of decoration with no substance. What that view overlooks is the possibility that it perhaps represented a great sigh of relief at escaping the fifties, the drab landscape of cities and ideas scarred in the aftermath of the war. Suddenly it seemed as if that it was not after all necessary to have forever to perpetuate a Dunkirk view of the world. Britten's 'War Requiem' in 1962 and the magnificent new Coventry Cathedral seemed to embody the spirit of reconciliation, an end to public mourning. If the decade was a wild party, for which we are now 'paying the price', then it was as necessary as the meal after a funeral, an acknowledgement that life must go on. It was also, I believe, symptomatic of a genuine change in social order; authority, in whatever form, no matter who held it, was no longer sacred, but constantly open to question – however much the holders of high office did (and do) try to evade accountability. In the midst of all the muddled thinking and the handing out of flowers by perfect strangers one to another it seemed for a while as if there was a spirit of greater democracy abroad, and few institutions have remained untouched by it. Some years before 'the media' became a singular noun, one of the television programmes that reflected this change was 'That Was the Week That Was', as savagely satirical for the time as a Scarfe cartoon is now. Its producer was Ned Sherrin and he, along with its stars, has remained a household name. Although the

*satirical edge has dulled a little with the years (the party's over) I am sure
he would be amused that the title of one of the pieces he chose for 'With
Great Pleasure' seems strangely topical – 'Of Hunting a Thatcher'.*

Sexey's school, where I was educated, provided me with an
introduction to the theatre. We went first to Stratford to see
Esmond Knight, who is now my next door neighbour in Chelsea,
in Peter Brook's *Winter's Tale* with Paul Scofield and Claire Bloom
in small parts, and then we used to go regularly to the Bristol Old
Vic where I distinctly remember one of Gertrude's breasts pop-
ping out in front of Robert Eddison's Hamlet. This was a bonus –
sex education thrown in – and the production had another
surprise for us. We'd been doing a little private sex educating at
school, handing round a 'dirty' book called *Cue for Passion*, and
when poor Hamlet came to his 'motive and cue for passion' line
the whole row of Sexey's schoolboys collapsed with guilty laughter. I often wonder when I see Robert Eddison in the King's Road,
if he tried without success to recapture that mysterious laugh on
subsequent performances. I don't think it would be a very good
idea if I were to read any Shakespeare. It would be a practical
rebuttal of my contention that the thing that surprised me at
school was to find that Shakespeare was such good money's
worth if you actually went to see the plays: and so Robin Phillips,
who is now a film actor and a distinguished stage director, and
who also started his career at the Bristol Old Vic School and in the
Bristol Old Vic Company, will read one of the sonnets.

Sonnet II
WILLIAM SHAKESPEARE

When forty winters shall besiege thy brow ·
And dig deep trenches in thy beauty's field,
Thy youth's proud livery, so gazed on now,
Will be a tatter'd weed, of small worth held:
Then being ask'd where all thy beauty lies,
Where all the treasure of thy lusty days,
To say, within thine own deep-sunken eyes,
Were an all-eating shame and thriftless praise.
How much more praise deserved thy beauty's use,

If thou could'st answer 'This fair child of mine
Shall sum my count and make my old excuse,'
Proving his beauty by succession thine!
This were to be new made when thou art old,
And see thy blood warm when thou feel'st it cold.

My mother has on her bookshelves a memorial edition of the works of Walter Raymond, a Somerset dialect novelist who died in 1931, and whose ashes are buried at Yeovil. He is now almost unknown outside Somerset and I have enjoyed introducing him to Christopher Fry and John Betjeman, and I was fiercely loyal to him as a boy, especially his two best books, the light and charming *Gemtleman Upcott's Daughter* – a sort of Queen Camel-and-Sparkford Romeo and Juliet (which I dramatised for the first radio play I ever wrote for the BBC's West Region) and the brooding *Two Men o' Mendip*. For me, Walter Raymond was always better than Thomas Hardy (though I'm prepared to believe that is local pride). I haven't been able to find a passage from either book that stands easily by itself, but here is a charming little essay which evokes very vividly for me the Somerset of my childhood.

Of Hunting a Thatcher
WALTER RAYMOND

So I had a cottage to thatch.

My landlord has been as good as his word, and the first load of reed was brought unexpectedly one morning soon after dawn on a 'long cart' that would otherwise have been passing empty on its way to the nearest town. How beautiful it looked, that pile of neat sheaves of wheaten reed, when first I saw it, with an easterly sunlight gilding one side and a deep purple brown shadow on the other! No sign of a cloud disturbed the serenity of a clear May sky, and it lay inside the garden hatch, beside the little brier-bush which smelt so sweet of a morning.

The villagers admired it as much as I. One said it was 'a very tidy lot o' reed', and another called it 'beaudivul', all ready for the thatcher when he should come.

I had selected a thatcher and written a line, but no word came in reply. This surprised nobody but myself. Only a week had elapsed, and in a country that never yields to the folly of hurry, what is a week? Besides, to be sure, no thatcher was ever out of a job. Thatchers were scarce. A man might go down on his bended knees to a thatcher and never get him to come.

The villagers took the liveliest interest in my doings; and man, woman, and child crowded at all hours to confer on my affairs. As yet I scarcely knew my neighbours. Only Mr Huckleston, the sexton, by reason of official position and force of character, stood out from the rest. He gazed at the reed and said, as though there might be a doubt of it: 'If you do really want a thatcher now, why don't ee take an' goo an' hunt vor un?'

The idea was charming.

All men are hunters – so much of the instinct of primitive man remains in each of us, that he who cannot traverse another continent to kill big game will sit in his easy chair and chase a rare postage stamp among the leaves of a catalogue.

I said I would start at once and obtain a thatcher by hunting.

Mr Huckleston was a little man, bald on the crown, but with long grey hair around his ears. He had run out without his hat, as the occasion required. He was solemn and precise, and his instructions were very minute.

'Wull,' said he, 'to thatcher's house is up six mile – but there, 'tidden his house, for he's a widder-man an' do bide wi' his married sister – an' 'tidden a step more, or not much more. 'Tis so straight's a gun-barrel all the way. When you do come up 'pon to o' the moor, you'll see a trackway to the right, but don't you take no notice o' he. You keep as you be a-gwaine. An' when you do come down by the beechen hedges, you'll see a lane turn off short to the left, but don't you take no notice o' he. And when you do come to the four cross-roads, don't you take no notice o' they, right or left, but keep on straight avore. The house is a stonen house, the first you do come to. An' if you do bear in mind what I have a-told ee, you can't make no mistake. An' there you had better to ax for Thatcher Tapp. An' then, if, as is likely, he do chance to be out, you'll hear.'

By close attention I managed to hit the way.

Over the broad moorland, where the wind rustling through the bare heather kept the air fresh and cool, even under the noonday sun; where larks sang overhead and pipits rose at every step, and, taking only a short flight, alighted again on the small patches of fine grass; where the curlews, just returned to their lonely nesting-ground by the moist places where rushes grow, whistled in alarm at the passing stranger. Truly, hunting a thatcher may lead a man amidst a thousand simple joys.

I found the stone house, but the thatcher was from home.

'He is away up to Littlemoor 'pon a job,' said the woman. 'He won't be home tonight. You could walk across an' catch un there.'

'How far is it?'

'May be five mile. May be six.'

'And did he get my letter?'

'He'll bear it in mind to see to it when he've a-got time to spare,' said she, with smiling, placid contentment.

But such an assurance gave me no comfort. That thatcher I must run down. I found the six miles came to eight in fact, for nobody here need make more than a guess at distance. I followed him to his place of work. He was thatching an old barn, or at least he had been. There was his thatcher's ladder stuck into the mossy old roof – there were his bat and hook, his reed and spars, but that thatcher himself was nowhere to be seen.

A man came slowly out of the 'barn's door'.

'I Thatcher Tapp? Dear no. He is but jus' gone. You could a'most catch un if you was to run. He's gone out by Littleford to hunt for a job. And 'tis on your road, too – or not so very much out.'

The scent was warm, and I went away, merrily. Not a soul, coming or going, was to be seen upon the lonely road. But at Littleford they all said boldly: 'What? Thatcher Tapp? There's no job for the man here. He ha'nt so mucha as showed his nose here.' Then, recognising the limitations of human knowledge, each one paused, shook his head solemnly, and added: 'Not's I know.'

So that thatcher was lost after all. There was nothing for it but to trudge home, quietly reflecting upon a remarkably good run.

When at last I reached my cottage I found a stranger sitting at ease upon the garden wall as if it belonged to him.

He stepped down in front of me and said: 'I be Thatcher Tapp. I've acomed about thik bit of a job. I've a-tookt a look round. 'Tis a tidy bit o' reed – beaudivul reed. I could come a-Monday.'

I could have embraced the man in my simple delight.

'Very well, then, Monday let it be,' I cried with alacrity.

But Monday came and no thatcher. Then Tuesday and Wednesday. On Thursday I determined to hunt again, and decided to draw Norton this time.

But all in vain. Two sons and a married daughter of the man who used to be there were still living in the place. The thatcher, however, was accounted amongst the extinct fauna of that delightful old town.

On my return I found Thatcher Tapp perched like a gigantic bird on the slope of my roof. He was busily at work. Already he had laid a golden strip upon the old sparrow-furrowed thatch.

The man's head was lifted above the ridge, and his sunburnt cheek glowed red against the blue sky. How tenderly he embraced the reed and laid it gently down to rest! How deftly he hammered in the spars with his bat, and trimmed the new thatch smooth with his thatcher's hook! The gable, the small square chimney, and the man made a picture wonderful in line and rich in colour. But all the primitive crafts are beautiful to watch.

Thus I hunted my thatcher.

How long will there be a thatcher to hunt?

Readers: Robin Phillips, Ned Sherrin

Full Selection:
The Old Curiosity Shop, CHARLES DICKENS
Sonnet II, WILLIAM SHAKESPEARE
Of Hunting a Thatcher, WALTER RAYMOND
Cricket Prints, FRANK WOOLLEY
Review of Augustin Daly's Production of a Midsummer Night's Dream, BERNARD SHAW
Essay on Dame Edith Evans – 'E' –, KENNETH TYNAN
New Year's Eve Poem 1965, PETER LEVI
A Consumer Guide to Religion, ROBERT GILLESPIE and CHARLES LEWSEN
No Bed for Bacon, CARYL BRAHMS and S.J. SIMON

NORMAN ST JOHN STEVAS

1984

Norman St John Stevas, once dubbed 'the acceptable face of Toryism', is a lover of the grand manner: few people after all, however religious, keep a harp in their living room. He asked and was able to arrange to have his programme recorded in the painted room at Chatsworth – a wonderful setting, but not exactly low key. However, another aspect of his character is one of elegant simplicity; his filing system, for example, consists of Harrods' bags tidily ranged on the floor around the walls of his study. His selection of items for the programme neatly reflected the driving passions of his life, politics and the Roman Catholic religion, leavened with an almost mischievous sense of humour.

The two great British contributions to world civilisation have been Parliamentary Government and English Literature. Now, one point at which these two interests meet, at least in my mind, is Mr Disraeli. The career of Disraeli can be summed up as a literary genius who applied that genius to politics. 'What,' asked Queen Victoria, 'What did Mr Disraeli really believe?' If she had wanted an answer she could have looked at the novels; there you find some very rich pickings. Fortunately for him, most of his colleagues in the Conservative party never read anything, so his secret was safe. His outstanding novels are, I think, *Coningsby* and *Sybil* – the latter the archetype of the social model. Disraeli knew about the poor, he knew their life much better than Dickens; he cared, he was concerned. The most famous dichotomy he made was between two nations. How relevant that is today, the divisions between north and south, between those in work and those out of it, the division summed up by the Bishop of Liverpool in that prophetic television broadcast between comfortable and suffering Britain. *Sybil* set out that contrast nearly a hundred and fifty years ago.

Sybil

BENJAMIN DISRAELI

'Well, society may be in its infancy,' said Egremont, slightly smiling; 'but say what you like, our Queen reigns over the greatest nation that ever existed.'

'Which nation?' asked the younger stranger, 'for she reigns over two.'

The stranger paused; Egremont was silent, but looked enquiringly.

'Yes,' resumed the younger stranger after a moment's interval, 'Two nations; between whom there is no intercourse and no sympathy; who are as ignorant of each other's habits, thoughts, and feelings, as if they were dwellers in different zones, or inhabitants of different planets; who are formed by a different breeding, are fed by a different food, are ordered by different manners, and are not governed by the same laws.'

'You speak of . . .' said Egremont hesitatingly.

'THE RICH AND THE POOR.'

'At this moment a sudden flush of rosy light, suffusing the grey ruins, indicated that the sun had just fallen; and, through a vacant arch that overlooked them, alone in the resplendent sky, glittered the twilight star.

Poetry is a deep thing and an elevating thing, the most surely wise and instructive of all the human things. Gerard Manley Hopkins is a poet's poet, but he was also a man of the spirit: a Jesuit who put his religious obedience ahead even of his genius. Where poetry is distinguished from prose is partly in rhythm and rhyme, but most of all I think in the concentration of images – and nowhere are the images denser than in Hopkins' poetry.

My choice is 'God's Grandeur'. I heard it recited in Westminster Cathedral by Dame Sybil Thorndike at a service for peace in Ireland. It was attended by both the Lord Chancellor and the Speaker of the House of Commons. And I read it myself at my mother's funeral.

I had a wonderful mother; she was adventurous, intrepid, witty, with a wonderful sense of fun. I remember, during her last illness, when she was in hospital, the matron came into her room – and matrons were matrons in those days. She was starched up to the eyeballs. My mother woke up at this moment, raised her hand into the air, and to my horror I heard her utter the single word, 'Waitress!' She realised that all was not well, said, 'A slip of the mind.' And went back to sleep. She was indomitable and I see something of her in this poem.

God's Grandeur
GERARD MANLEY HOPKINS

The world is charged with the grandeur of God.
　It will flame out, like shining from shook foil;
　It gathers to a greatness, like the ooze of oil
Crushed. Why do men then now not reck his rod?
Generations have trod, have trod, have trod;
　And all is seared with trade; bleared, smeared with toil;
　And wears man's smudge and shares man's smell: the soil
Is bare now, nor can foot feel, being shod.

And for all this, nature is never spent;
　There lives the dearest freshness deep down things;
And though the last lights off the black West went
　Oh, morning, at the brown brink eastward, springs –
Because the Holy Ghost over the bent
　World broods with warm breast and with ah! bright
　　wings.

Most of us have a no clear visual ideal of God. We are left with the stern judge or the man with the beard or the angry old man. To create an antidote to all this pernicious nonsense we have Mother Julian of Norwich, her 'Revelations of Divine Love'. Across the centuries comes her message which she wrote down 600 years ago.

Revelations of Divine Love
JULIAN OF NORWICH

It was at this time that our Lord showed me spiritually how intimately he loves us. I saw that he is everything that we know to be good and helpful. In his love he clothes us, enfolds and embraces us; that tender love completely surrounds us, never to leave us. As I saw it he is everything that is good.

And he showed me more, a little thing, the size of a hazel-nut, on the palm of my hand, round like a ball. I looked at it thoughtfully and wondered, 'What is this?' And the answer came, 'It is all that is made.' I marvelled that it continued to exist and did not suddenly disintegrate; it was so small. And again my mind supplied the answer, 'It exists, both now and forever, because God loves it.' In short, everything owes its existence to the love of God.

Readers: Jill Balcon, Michael Hordern

Full Selection:
Sybil, BENJAMIN DISRAELI
Ballade of Illegal Ornaments, HILAIRE BELLOC
Mapp and Lucia, E. F. BENSON
God's Grandeur, GERARD MANLEY HOPKINS
The Prince, MACHIAVELLI
Anthem for Doomed Youth, WILFRED OWEN
Revelations of Divine Love, JULIAN OF NORWICH
The Green Carnation, HITCHENS
On Shakespeare, WALTER BAGEHOT
King Lear Act 5, Scene 3, WILLIAM SHAKESPEARE
Sense and Sensibility, JANE AUSTEN
The More Loving One, AUDEN
To Hope, JOHN KEATS

DORIAN WILLIAMS

1982

At the beginning of the programme Dorian Williams gently mocked the idea that just because his professional life is taken up with things horsey he has no interest in other things, like reading. By displaying a sensitive and deeply humorous personality he proved his point for those who should have known better, including, I must confess, myself, and, I suspect Brian Patten who produced the programme. It confirmed what I have discovered again and again – that whatever view of the person I may have formed before meeting and working on this programme, I very soon discover that it was a one-sided impression and that the presenters are always more complicated, more interesting and more likeable than their public face would suggest.

This is really a wonderful opportunity for me to wear another hat because I find that most people think, and perhaps understandably, that I am entirely associated with horses – in fact I often say that whenever I am introduced to speak at some function people expect half a horse to get up. I'm never sure which half, but perhaps that doesn't matter. Anyway it is true that I come from a horsey background, my parents in fact were really more or less founders of the Pony Club and my father was very much associated with the beginning of the British Show Jumping Association. But although my background is horsey, I have always enjoyed reading and as a small child I loved being read to aloud. I particularly enjoyed learning by heart. I loved the great epics and when I learned at prep school some of those great epics by heart I was probably the only boy in the school that really enjoyed it, but I did. In fact, at the age of thirteen I think I knew just about the whole of John Masefield's 'Right Royal' by heart. I always preferred it to the more famous 'Reynard the Fox' and I still think that in addition to the thrill of the race – it is, in fact, a fictitious description of the Grand National – it had real poetry in it and something of the magic that John Masefield used to bring to his poems about the sea.

Right Royal
JOHN MASEFIELD

And now, beyond question, the field began tailing,
For all had been tested and many were ailing,
The riders were weary, the horses were failing,
The blur of bright colours rolled over the railing,
With grunts of urged horses, and the oaths of hot men,
'Gerr on, you', 'Come on, now', agen and agen;
They spattered the mud on the willow tree's bole
And they charged at the danger; and the danger took toll.

For Monkery landed, but dwelt on the fence,
So the Counter Vair passed him in galloping thence.
Then Stormalong blundered, then bright Muscatel
Slipped badly on landing and stumbled and fell,
With his whip in the mud and his stirrups both gone,
Yet he kept in the saddle and made him go on.

As Charles leaped the Turn, all the field was tailed out
Like petals of roses that wind blows about,
Like petals of colour blown back and brought near,
Like poppies in wind-flaws when corn is in ear;
Fate held them or sped them, the race was beginning.
Charles said, 'I must ride, or I've no chance of winning.'

Charles Cottill was of course the hero, who despite a fall caught up and won on the post.

As a teenager I was attempting to write poetry myself, most of it, I'm afraid, showing all too clearly the influence of Will Ogilvy, that great hunting poet whose marvellous books such as *Scattered Scarlet, Galloping Shoes* and *Over the Grass* were always welcome at

Christmas. One day at school we were set to write a poem with the title of 'Tranquillity'. In the same house as myself was Terence Rattigan, with whom I was quite friendly, and in discussing the matter with him, because he was already proving himself an extremely talented writer, he suggested that I should write a poem about a cat – I am sure I would have preferred a dog or a horse, but perhaps a cat *is* rather more tranquil. All went well until the last two lines or possibly the whole of the last verse, which very obligingly Terry supplied: so at last he's getting due credit, and he was probably responsible for my poem appearing in the school magazine – my first appearance in print.

Tranquillity
DORIAN WILLIAMS

The room was quaintly lit, the firelight flicking
   The gloom with lash of flame.
Over the hearth, the clock was slowly ticking
   A song without a name.

An old man lay, in seas of slumber drifting,
   Remote and free from care;
On softened face the glow, forever drifting,
   Trembled, and on his hair.

A cat dozed, purring, by the tranquil sleeper,
   Lay, purring, dimly seen,
While shadows mingled deeper yet and deeper;
   Her half-closed eyes shone green.

And now, in drowsy peace, the cat crept nearer
   Her master's slippered feet,
And still her crooning, for her far-off hearer
   Lay lost in failing heat.

The embers, dying, dropped, their death was creeping;
   The last red spark had leapt;
Yet still those placid dreamers went on sleeping,
   And slept and slept and slept.

When one is very young one loves the illogical, nonsense, rubbish, everything exaggerated and eccentric. In adolescence one becomes very logical and one can neither understand nor accept anything that is illogical or nonsensical. In adulthood once again appreciates the joy of the illogical and so it is I believe that small children love *Alice in Wonderland*, adolescents just cannot take it, but adults, if they are lucky return to it and then fully appreciate the remarkable genius of Lewis Carroll. Here is a short passage from *Through the Looking Glass* which is, perhaps particularly appropriate, as it is a passage where the White Knight finds it very easy to fall off – but greatly resents being told that he needs more practice – another common fault in riders!

The White Knight from
Alice through the looking glass
LEWIS CARROLL

Whenever the horse stopped (which it did very often), he fell off in front; and, whenever it went on again (which it generally did rather suddenly), he fell off behind. Otherwise he kept on pretty well, except that he had a habit of now and then falling off sideways; and as he generally did this on the side on which Alice was walking, she soon found that it was the best plan not to walk *quite* close to the horse.

'I'm afraid you've not had much practice in riding,' she ventured to say, as she was helping him up from his fifth tumble.

The Knight looked very much surprised, and a little offended at the remark. 'What makes you say that?' he asked, as he scrambled back into the saddle, keeping hold of Alice's hair with one hand, to save himself from falling over on the other side.

'Because people don't fall off quite so often, when they've had much practice.'

'I've had plenty of practice,' the Knight said very gravely: 'plenty of practice!'

Alice could think of nothing better to say than 'Indeed?' but she said it as heartily as she could. They went on a little way in silence after this, the Knight with his eyes shut, muttering to himself, and Alice watching anxiously for the next tumble.

'The great art of riding,' the Knight suddenly began in a loud voice, waving his right arm as he spoke, 'is to keep –' Here the sentence ended as suddenly as it had begun, as the Knight fell heavily on the top of his head exactly in the path where Alice was walking. She was quite frightened this time, and said in an anxious tone, as she picked him up, 'I hope no bones are broken?'

'None to speak of,' the Knight said, as if he didn't mind breaking two or three of them. 'The great art of riding, as I was saying, is – to keep your balance properly. Like this, you know –'

He let go the bridle, and stretched out both his arms to show Alice what he meant, and this time he fell flat on his back, right under the horse's feet.

'Plenty of practice!' he went on repeating, all the time that Alice was getting him on his feet again. 'Plenty of practice!'

'It's too ridiculous!' cried Alice, losing all her patience this time. 'You ought to have a wooden horse on wheels, that you ought!'

'Does that kind go smoothly?' the Knight asked in a tone of great interest, clasping his arms round the horse's neck as he spoke, just in time to save himself from tumbling off again.

'Much more smoothly than a live horse,' Alice said, with a little scream of laughter, in spite of all she could do to prevent it.

'I'll get one,' the Knight said thoughtfully to himself. 'One or two – several.'

Readers: Richard Johnson, Joyce Redman

Full Selection:
Horatius, LORD MACAULAY
Right Royal, JOHN MASEFIELD
Tranquillity, DORIAN WILLIAMS
Ode to a Nightingale, JOHN KEATS
Kilvert's Diary, REV. FRANCIS KILVERT
Alice Through the Looking Glass, LEWIS CARROLL
A Shropshire Lad, A. E. HOUSMAN
Brendon Hill, A. E. HOUSMAN
Handley Cross, R. S. SURTEES
Hunter Trials, JOHN BETJEMAN
Venus Observed, CHRISTOPHER FRY
Henry V, WILLIAM SHAKESPEARE
East Coker, T. S. ELIOT

INDEX